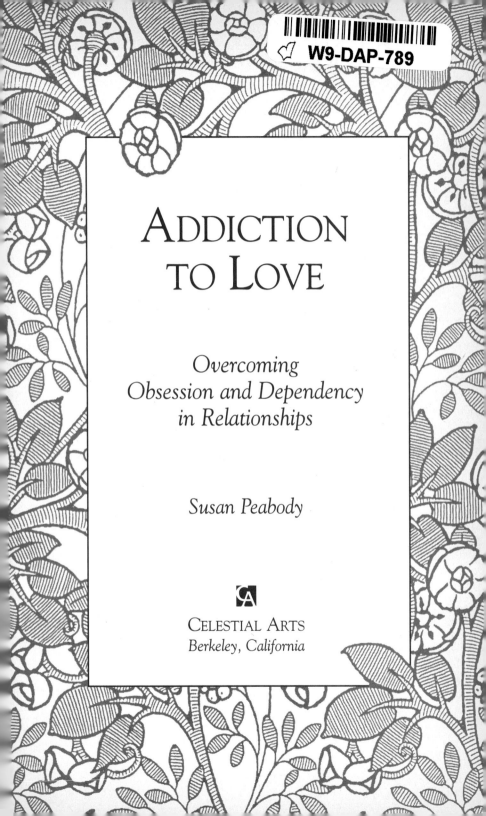

ADDICTION TO LOVE

*Overcoming
Obsession and Dependency
in Relationships*

Susan Peabody

CELESTIAL ARTS
Berkeley, California

ACKNOWLEDGMENTS

I would like to thank the following people
for helping me along the way:
Kathleen Peabody, Barry Morgan, Jerry Kramer, Meridith Murphy,
Michael Steele, Ethel Swank, Elsa Tuxler, Bonnie Jacobs,
Clyde Wallace, Cheryl Leslie, Nancy Morris, Joan Roland,
Giuseppe Rensi, Dana Ogden, Linda Beauvais and David Hinds.

Cover & text design by Nancy Austin and Toni Tajima

FIRST CELESTIAL ARTS PRINTING 1994

Library of Congress Cataloging-in-Publication Data
Peabody, Susan, 1948-
Addiction to love / by Susan Peabody.
p. cm.
Bibliography: p.
ISBN 0-89087-715-7:
1. Relationship addiction. I. Title.
RC552.R44R43 1989
616.85'227--DC19 88-38975
CIP

3   4   5   6   /   99   98

To my daughter Kathy,
whose unconditional love
always gives me strength;

to my son Karl
who taught me that it's all right to dream
as long as you know how to
"let go and let God;"

and to my students
who have taught me everything anyone
would ever want to know about
addiction to love—

God bless you all!

Contents

PREFACE TO THE SECOND EDITION   ix

PREFACE TO THE FIRST EDITION   xi

INTRODUCTION   xv

I. LOOKING FOR LOVE
    The Hungry Heart   3

II. THE MANY FORMS OF ADDICTION
    TO LOVE

    Fatal Attraction, Casanova,
       and Stand By Your Man   11

    Addictions to Parents, Children,
       Siblings, or Friends   13

    Two-way Addictions   14

    Obsessing About an Unavailable Person   15

    Becoming Dependent on an Abusive Partner   17

    Dual and Subsidiary Addictions   21

    Obsessions That Go Underground   23

    Hurting Others   24

    Crimes of the Heart   25

III. CONTRIBUTING FACTORS THAT INFLUENCE POTENTIAL LOVE ADDICTS

Contributing Factors   31

Love Songs and Myths About Romantic Love   31

Role Structuring   33

Inadequate Role Models   34

IV. SYMPTOMS OF ADDICTION TO LOVE AND SUGGESTIONS FOR CHANGE

Love at First Sight   37

Excessive Fantasizing   38

The Need to Create Drama and Excitement   40

Exaggerated Fears in Relationships   43

Abnormal Jealousy   45

Dysfunctional Emotions   46

Weak Personality Boundaries   49

High Level of Tolerance for Suffering in Relationships   50

Accepting Dishonesty   51

Being Ruled By Your Libido   54

Confusing Need with Want   55

The Compelling Need to Control   55

Image Management   56

Nagging   58

Being Helpless   59

Projecting Guilt   60

Stimulating Jealousy   60

Flattery   61

The Silent Treatment   62

Sex   62

Negative Caretaking   63
An Attack of Hysteria or Rage   66

V. THE PROGRESSION OF ADDICTION
  TO LOVE
    Contributing Factors   71
    Beginning Stage   71
    Chronic State   72
    Dying for Love   72
    Typical Progression   72

VI. RECOVERY
    Courageously Facing Your Own Shortcomings   83
    Making Changes   85
    Progress Not Perfection   87
    Therapy and Support Groups Really Do Help   90
    Healing the Wounds of Childhood Trauma   93
    The Eternal Child Within   99
    Building Self-Esteem   102
    Spirituality and Recovery   106
    Christian Ideals   114
    Can an Addictive Relationship be Saved?   118
    Ending a Relationship When It Is Necessary   119
    Being Single   123

VII. STARTING OVER AGAIN
    Personality Types That Trigger Addictive
      Behavior   127
    The Love Addict   128
    The Narcissist   129
    The Fear of Intimacy Underlying the
      Yearning to be Loved   129

Hidden Signals 132
Picking Up the Signals 140

VIII. CREATING LOVING AND FULFILLING RELATIONSHIPS
The Ingredients of a Healthy Relationship 143
The Progression of a Healthy Relationship 146

APPENDICES
Worksheet #1–Am I a Love Addict? 155
Worksheet #2–An Inventory of My Unhealthy Relationships 158
Worksheet #3–Am I Ready for a Healthy Relationship? 162
Worksheet #4–Do I Have a Healthy Relationship? 165
A Summary of the Addiction Process 167
Inner-Child Meditation 171
The 12 Steps to Recovery 175
Support Group Meeting Format 181
Suggested Reading 185

Preface to the Second Edition

Since the publication of *Addiction to Love* in 1989, I have been asked a lot of questions about "loving too much." People are hungry for information about this subject.

In response to these questions, I am introducing an expanded edition of *Addiction to Love*. It is meant to clarify concepts already discussed and to provide new information. Section II is new. It discusses more fully the many forms of addiction to love. There is more variety than you might think. Some love addicts are addicted to romance while others are hooked on a person or a relationship.

The progression of addiction to love is also discussed more fully in Section V, and I have added a lengthy description of a typical love addict—a composite of myself and some of my students.

The most important part of this new edition is the section on recovery. This has been expanded the most. I now offer more detailed information about changing, transcending childhood trauma, reparenting and spirituality; and I have also added a chapter addressing the special needs of the Christian love addict.

To a certain extent the first edition of *Addiction to Love* left people hanging when it came to starting over. This time around I have a lot more to say about what a healthy relationship is.

Finally, the appendices in this edition includes some worksheets you might find helpful as well as an inner child meditation; a support group format; a description of the twelve steps for those who attend 12-step meetings; and a list of more books than you could ever read in a lifetime. (I have only read about a fourth of them. The others have been recommended by my students.)

I hope everyone finds this new edition of *Addiction to Love* helpful, and my best to everyone who is struggling with this very painful disorder. Never give up trying to get better!

Susan Peabody
January, 1994

Preface to the First Edition

I first became interested in the subject of obsessive behavior in relationships when Robin Norwood released her book *Women Who Love Too Much*. Needless to say, I recognized many of my own obsessive behavior patterns, and coincidentally I was ready to make major changes in my life along the lines she suggested.

Enthusiastic, and ready to get help, I looked around for a support group. Unfortunately, there were no "Women Who Love Too Much" support groups in my area. Undaunted, I started my own meeting for women who wanted to deal with the issues introduced by Robin Norwood. This seemed like a great way to promote my own recovery and at the same time offer other women the opportunity to turn their lives around.

A year after the group began, when I was about a mile down the road to recovery (according to Robin Norwood's chart), I became interested in teaching others about the "disease" of "loving too much." Armed with a teaching credential, a desire to be instrumental in helping others, and the support of all my friends, I approached the principal of a local adult school. He was very enthusiastic about the general subject matter of the course I wanted to teach, but he encouraged me not to limit myself to just the issues presented in Robin Norwood's book. He also wanted me to allow men in my class. When I agreed, he suggested I call my course "Addiction to Love."

Excited about the challenge of teaching "Addiction to Love," I set aside Robin Norwood's book for awhile and began reading other literature about obsessive behavior in relationships. This, of course, was a great learning experience for me. I was amazed to find out how much had been written about love, obsession, and dependency. (Even Kierkergaard, as far back as the 1840's, wrote about the "habitual" nature of romantic love. See *Works of Love*.)

Once I had acquired a lot of professional information about love and addiction (information which I could use to supplement what I had learned from my own personal experiences and the experiences of the women in my support group), I began to prepare an outline for my course. My goal was to condense and clarify many of the ideas introduced by others, and then to interject some of my own concepts. By my own concepts I mean an analysis of my own experiences. For example, in addressing the question of why some people become obsessive in relationships and others don't, most authors get around to discussing the debilitating effects of childhood deprivation within the dysfunctional home. Yet, none of them mention the devastating effects of peer rejection and how it relates to the creation of a lonely, needy love addict. Since this was a big issue in my life I felt it was important to explore it a little further. Also, none of the authors discuss the relationship between fantasizing and "addiction to love." To me, this is like talking about baking bread and forgetting to mention the yeast. Having been addicted to fantasizing, as well as romantic love, I knew the connection between the two needed to be considered.

When I finally had what I thought was a model of a course about "Addiction to Love," I taught my first class. It was an exhilarating experience, and the response of my students really made it clear that I had put together some valuable information about a very serious problem. This is what prompted me to put my course outline in manuscript form and make it available to people who, for various reasons, could not take the class.

Since *Addiction to Love* first became available, I have gotten a positive response from everyone who reads it. People seem to appreciate the simplified concepts about obsessing in relationships and the "Suggestions for Change." Of course, I am very appreciative of this response and happy to be contributing in this way. Most of all, I am glad to be recovering from this disorder myself and able to offer the following message. If you are a love addict, you are not alone. There is hope and there is recovery. If you have suffered enough, and are ready to make certain changes, you can follow in my footsteps and those of other recovering love addicts. You can have a brighter tomorrow.

Introduction

All addictions have one thing in common. In the beginning stages they are an attempt to control pleasure and pain by inducing experiences that (1) alleviate boredom; (2) promote a feeling of well-being; and (3) provide an escape from pain and sorrow. The only difference between one addiction and another is the hook or the experience which helps the addict manage life's highs and lows. For example, with alcoholism this hook is either the personality change that comes with getting drunk (the escape from one's self or the release of inhibitions), or the anesthetizing affects of alcohol (its ability to deaden painful feelings). With drug addiction the hook is the mind-altering experience of getting high (an escape from boredom, reality and/or pain). With workaholism the hook is the distraction that comes from focused concentration on an activity. With overeating it is the unconscious association between food and nurturing (this alleviates the emotional pain that comes from one's infantile fear of abandonment); and with sex-addiction the hook is the experience of escaping into a euphoric high stimulated by sexual activity.

When it comes to love we have two different hooks (1) romantic fantasies which help deaden feelings of loneliness and rejection by promising "happiness ever after" (hope for the future); and (2) the experience of attachment or bonding which abates our conscious and unconscious fear of abandonment and falsely promises to eliminate, diminish, or at least compensate for loneliness and low self-esteem.

While the hook which draws the love addict into the addiction process is unique, the progression of the disorder is not. Once hooked, the addict experiences a euphoric beginning followed by a decline in the reinforcing effects of the addiction, and the eventual emergence of all the life-threatening problems associated with dependency. This is the dark side of romantic love and relationships. This is pain and suffering at its worst, and for many unfortunate men and women this is the story of their lives.

Therefore worldly prudence shouts early and late: look before you love.

SØREN KIERKEGAARD in *Works of Love*

I.

LOOKING FOR LOVE

Poets have no right to picture love as blind; its blindfold must be removed so that it can have the use of eyes.

PASCAL as quoted by Jose Ortega y Gasset
in *On Love*

THE HUNGRY HEART

The heart is a lonely hunter.

CARSON MCCULLERS

Being obsessed with a person or a relationship, and calling that obsession love, is a phenomenon that is finally being recognized as a pervasive and serious problem. Anne Schaef, in her book *Co-dependence: Misunderstood, Mistreated*, gives us an informative look at what the mental health field calls "co-dependence" (obsessing about an alcoholic or chemically dependent partner). Robin Norwood takes obsessing in relationships out of the realm of substance abuse by directing our attention to the heartbreaking dilemma of "loving too much." Finally, in their analysis of this phenomenon, Howard Halpern, in "How to Break an Addiction to a Person," and Stanton Peele, in "Love and Addiction," not only explain the origins of obsessive behavior in relationships, they point out that this behavior is symptomatic of an addiction.

Halpern and Peele have a point. Obsessing about a person or a relationship *is* symptomatic of an addiction. To clarify this point further, let me explain how the addiction process works. It all begins with what seems like an innocent attraction to someone, which quickly turns into an infatuation (idealizing

3

someone you don't know very well). The potential love addict, who is insecure and hungry for love, takes this infatuation much too seriously and easily becomes blinded by the exhilarating effects of "love at first sight." (By "blinded" I mean incapable of being practical or unable to avoid potentially unhealthy situations.)

Once Cupid has hit his mark, the soon-to-be love addict quickly becomes excessively preoccupied with the loved one. Every other aspect of his or her life becomes less important than this new lover, and endless hours are spent fantasizing about how the relationship is going to develop. Of course, to a certain extent we all go through this when we fall in love, but with the love addict there is no holding back or common sense. Responsible behavior flies out the window and everybody and everything takes a back seat to this new relationship. (For those who think this is normal behavior, think again. Even if romantic love is blossoming, it is not healthy to turn your life upside down and become a slave to your feelings.)

At about this point, love addicts will project onto the loved one all of their dreams for eternal happiness via the reinforcing effects of romantic love. Of course, someone who is emotionally secure realizes that one person cannot be totally responsible for another person's happiness, but love addicts (who are looking for someone to "fix" them) don't comprehend this idea, and they proceed to pin all of their hopes for happiness on this one person. (To one degree or another, we all fall victim to the illusion that someone else is responsible for our happiness, but love addicts cling to this idea as if it were a life or death situation. They are totally convinced that their happiness lies in the hands of someone else and life for them is just an endless search for the holder of their dreams.)

Once the love addict has projected all of his or her dreams for happiness onto the new lover (unconsciously making the decision that *only* this person can make him or her happy), the dependency stage of the addiction is triggered and with it the love addict's deep-seated fear that the relationship will end and his or her dreams will be smashed. At this point, with so much at stake, a pattern of obsessive behavior emerges. This pattern is designed to ensure that the relationship survives. That is, the love addict will now start trying to control his or her partner as a self-defeating way of holding on. The particulars will vary with each relationship, but the goal is the same. Hold on at any cost to this person, this relationship, this dream.

This is the stage at which the relationship usually begins to deteriorate. This is because while the love addict is putting forth so much energy to keep the relationship alive, his or her partner is usually reacting to this in a negative way. Depending on the individual and the situation, the love addict's partner will now begin to feel smothered, overburdened, intimidated, angry, and/or ungrateful. (In some cases, he or she will also feel free to become increasingly selfish, demanding, dishonest, neglectful or abusive, i.e., take advantage of the love addict.) Of course, this puts more stress on the relationship and the love addict tries even harder to hold things together. This further erodes the relationship and a vicious cycle begins.

The hallmark of an addictive relationship is the fact that this deterioration does not mean the end of the union. Because love addicts are dependent on their relationships to keep their dreams of happiness alive, they are far from ready to give up so easily. Instead, they work out an increasingly elaborate network of denial so they can pretend nothing is wrong. This is very sad. "Diminishing returns" would discourage other people, but a real love addict holds on even tighter. It's sort of like hanging onto a live wire. It hurts, but you can't let go.

Eventually, the stress of all this will take its toll, and the love addict's emotional and physical well-being will start to deteriorate along with the relationship. Stress related disorders become chronic and other obsessions (food, alcohol, drugs) become a tempting way to dull the pain. This is the final stage of the addiction and often the turning point. This is when the relationship usually explodes or falls apart.

Unfortunately, the end of one addictive relationship is not always the end of the love addict's battle with this emotional problem. For many sufferers, this way of relating to others is a pattern in their lives, and when one addictive relationship ends another just begins. In time the resiliency of the person who loves addictively will decrease and their physical and emotional ailments will become life-threatening. They may even die. As Robin Norwood puts it, "...I want to reiterate that loving too much can kill you." It is this phenomenon of "dying for love" which particularly validates Halpern's and Peele's assertion that obsessing about a person in the name of love is symptomatic of an addiction. Anyone who holds onto something at the risk of their own life is addicted.

At this point the reader may be asking why some people are so needy and insecure that they get caught up in the devastating effects of an addictive relationship. Where does this insatiable hunger for love come from? Most experts agree that it is a by-product of childhood deprivation, but opinions differ as to which type of deprivation does the most damage.

Howard Halpern declares that the roots of addiction to love can be traced to what he calls an overwhelming "attachment hunger." Halpern explains that "attachment hunger" is our natural need to attach or bond to someone—a need which stems from our unconscious desire to recreate the euphoric feelings of peace and omnipotence that we experienced as infants when we were totally dependent on our mothers. While most people have a normal or typical "attachment hunger" which causes little pain and blossoms into a normal desire to become intimate with another human being, some have an overwhelming "attachment hunger" which has the power to distort reality and lead to obsessive behavior in relationships.

Halpern goes on to say that whether or not a person has an overwhelming "attachment hunger" depends on how that person's dependency bond with their mother was broken. If the feelings of safety and euphoria were interrupted in a healthy way, the child felt secure in their independence and not as if they had been cut adrift from their life-giving source. If the dependency bond was broken prematurely, insensitively, or sadistically, the child did not have time to adjust and he or she was left with an overwhelming "attachment hunger." As a result, when these children become adults they feel an especially strong need to bond to someone. They unconsciously equate being in a relationship with survival—they think they will die of loneliness if they are not involved with someone. If this feeling is strong enough, this person will do anything to hold onto someone they have become attached to. They will obsess and they will become addicted.

While a traumatic rift in the dependency bond certainly explains why some people so easily turn an attachment (or love) into an addiction, it does not take into consideration the more ravaging effects of growing up in a dysfunctional home. According to Robin Norwood, this is where the seeds of addictive loving are sown. She explains that in a dysfunctional home (a family environment which is not conducive to the mental and physical well-being of the family members), children are neglected or abused over a long period of time and deprived of the kind of attention, strokes, and role-modeling they need to become healthy, well-adjusted adults capable of loving normally. She makes it clear that children who grow up under these conditions are operating with a handicap and tend to "love too much" or become addicted to love.

Of course, Norwood and Halpern are both right. "Attachment hunger" and growing up in a dysfunctional home do explain the connection between childhood deprivation and loving addictively. However, I would like to add one more thought to their insights. Many love addicts can also trace their neediness and feelings of inadequacy back to those painful years when they were "wall flowers," or on the outside looking in; and like an overwhelming "attachment hunger" and growing up in a dysfunctional home, peer rejection and feeling left out can deprive children of the nurturing benefits of acceptance and the natural growth of self-esteem which could help them become healthy, well-adjusted adults able to seek and find love in a normal way.

With most love addicts peer rejection is linked to parental deprivation. That is, children growing up in a dysfunctional home might experience peer rejection because other children react negatively to their emotional problems (very often children who are unloved at home are emotionally unstable, and therefore unsociable, fearful, antagonistic, pushy, too anxious to please, etc.). However, in some cases peer rejection is not linked to problems at home. That is, even if a child does receive parental love in a "normal" home environment they may still experience peer rejection because they are shy, self-conscious, disfigured, plain, too bright, overweight, come from a low-income home, have difficulty relating to others or just don't fit in where they happen to be growing up. Of course, in either case the impact of peer rejection is relatively the same. It tends to make a child insecure and hungry for acceptance.

Few children can escape the after-effects of an unhealthy interruption of the dependency bond, the lack of proper parental nurturing, or inadequate interactions with their peers. Instead they grow up lacking in self-esteem and hungry for love. This, in turn, predisposes them to become love addicts or to become easily obsessed with someone who holds for them the promise of "living happily ever after" by way of "true love"—even when they find out that a kiss never really awakens Sleeping Beauty or turns a frog into a prince.

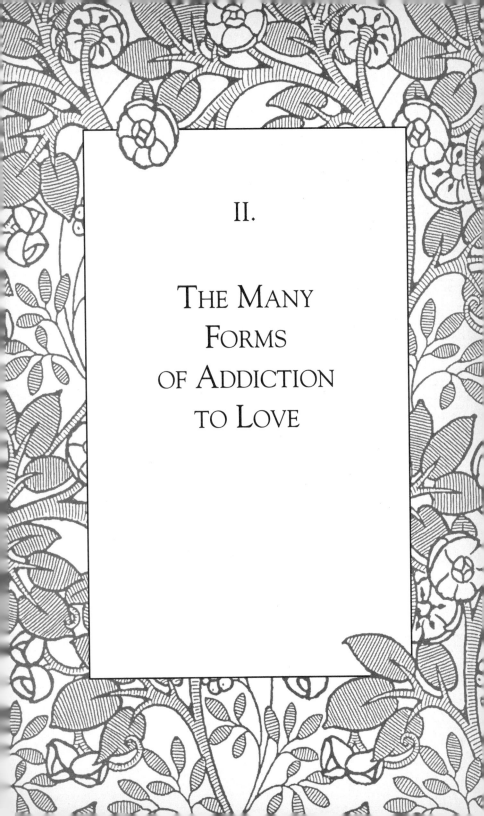

II.

THE MANY FORMS OF ADDICTION TO LOVE

How do I love thee? Let me count the ways.

ELIZABETH BARRETT BROWNING
in *Sonnets from the Portuguese*

FATAL ATTRACTION, CASANOVA, AND STAND BY YOUR MAN

Spontaneous [romantic] love makes a man free and in the next moment dependent... spontaneous love can become unhappy, can reach the point of despair.

SØREN KIERKEGAARD in *Works of Love*

Love addicts are preoccupied in an unhealthy way with either a person, a relationship, or romance. The movie Fatal Attraction illustrates the plight of the love addict obsessed with a person. Glen Close is obsessed with Michael Douglas. She has to have him or die trying.

Other love addicts are more addicted to the idea of being in a relationship than they are to any particular person. I call these people *relationship* addicts and there are two types. There are the relationship addicts who can easily let go of their partner, but they can't conceive of themselves as being without someone. Therefore, when a relationship ends, these love addicts quickly involve themselves with someone else. (Often they have someone waiting in the wings.) Then, there are the relationship addicts who cling to their partner no matter what —even if they don't love him or her. The mantra of this type of love addict is, "I hate you don't leave me" or "Stand by your man." However, it is important to note that these love addicts are not really obsessed with their partner; they are addicted to the relationship and will hold on to it until they find someone else to be their partner.

Some love addicts are not addicted to either a person or a relationship. They are addicted to romance—the chemistry of romantic love (what Kierkegaard calls erotic or preferential love). Romance addicts place a high priority on sexual attraction because they are getting high off of the passion, and when the passion diminishes they move on. Romance addicts can also be overly preoccupied with romantic rituals such as dating, candlelight dinners, romantic settings, i.e. a weekend at a bed and breakfast—any romantic interaction that is a manifestation of their childhood fantasies about romance.

Romance addicts don't really want a fully developed relationship, they want romance. For instance, I know women who only get involved with married men because an affair is much more exciting than a real relationship or because they see forbidden love as romantic. The men I know who are addicted to romance never get past the first stages of a relationship. Their excuse for never settling down is that they are looking for the perfect woman, but in reality they are just hooked on the passion they can only feel when they first meet someone.

Romance addicts may experience the illusion of falling in love with a person, or they may even have a brief relationship with someone who can help them act out their fantasies, but their focus is on the romance not the relationship since both the person and the relationship are secondary to their need for romantic stimuli.

While some people experience just one form of addiction to love, others switch from one to another. Take the example of a love addict who becomes addicted to her lover after a whirlwind romance. At some point the relationship begins to deteriorate and the love addict no longer finds her partner attractive. So she stops obsessing about him. However, this is not the end of her addiction. She just switches gears and becomes dependent on the partnership. She isn't in love anymore, but she clings to the reinforcing effects of the relationship. Maybe she is financially dependent on her partner or she finds the routine of the relationship comfortable. Maybe she feels that being with someone she doesn't love is better than being alone. Whatever her reasons, she has switched from being addicted to a person to being dependent on the relationship. The players have not changed, but her addiction has.

ADDICTIONS TO PARENTS, CHILDREN, SIBLINGS OR FRIENDS

Entreat her not to leave you or to return from
following you; for where you go I will go and
where you lodge I will lodge...where you die
I will die.

RUTH to her mother-in-law Naomi
in Ruth 6:16-17

Now and then, I meet people who tell me they are not addicted to a lover, but to a friend, parent, child, or sibling. This brings up an important point. Is an unhealthy dependency always tied to romantic love? No, it is not. Sometimes the yearning to love, and be loved, gets split off from romantic ideals and projected onto anyone the love addict feels close to. Then, the addictive process proceeds in much the same manner. The hunger for love becomes a preoccupation with the loved one. This becomes an obsession which later develops into an unhealthy dependency and addiction.

I have known people who were addicted to their parents. They could not leave home after they had grown up, or they had to call their parents every day to feel comfortable. One of my male students was addicted to his mother. She had raised him as a single parent after getting divorced from his father. After he grew up he continued to live at home. When he was thirty-five his mother tried to remarry. He flew into a rage and told her he would never speak to her again.

I have known people who were too dependent on their children, letting them become the focus of their whole life. Such parents cannot accept their children's independence. Once I was doing a radio show to promote the first edition of this book and I got a call from a listener who said his mother was addicted to him. He said she called him every day, sent him money he didn't ask for, and gave him non-stop, unsolicited advice. He said her attempts to control him were beyond belief and that she didn't seem to be interested in anything but his life.

One of my female students told me that she was addicted to both her mother and her sister. At forty, Jane was still living with her mother and younger sister. She didn't have any friends or outside interests. Both her mother and sister were able-bodied, but neither one of them did anything to bring money into the home or help with the housework. Jane was their caretaker and provider. She felt responsible for them and sacrificed her life rather than face her dependency.

TWO-WAY ADDICTIONS

*All through the dark...they gave themselves
up to love. Apart the lovers could neither live
nor die, for it was life and death together.
They lived on roots and herbs and the flesh of
wild animals. Their skin stretched tight over*

their thin bodies, they were pallid and their clothes were ragged. But they gazed at one another...and they did not know they suffered.

> ROBERT JOHNSON in *We: Understanding the Psychology of Romantic Love*, about the romance of Tristan and Isolde as retold by Joseph Bedier

Many people see the phenomenon of addiction to love as one person obsessing while the other person is running away. This is not always true. Two people can be addicted to each other. I call this a two-way addiction.

Two-way addictions are glorified in this culture. After all, Romeo and Juliet died rather than live without each other. However, in my opinion, two-way addictions are unhealthy. This is because the lovers are totally dependent on one another. Their partnership is a life or death matter. They have fallen in love overnight, begun fantasizing excessively about each other, and allowed the relationship to be the only focus of their life. Addicted lovers feel all the dysfunctional emotions associated with obsession. This includes intense jealousy and an abnormal fear of abandonment. There is also a lot of controlling, and neither partner is developing as an individual.

OBSESSING ABOUT AN UNAVAILABLE PERSON

Does the imagination dwell the most upon a woman won or a woman lost?

> WILLIAM BUTLER YEATS in *The Tower*

Many love addicts find they have a history of falling in love with an unavailable person and they wonder why this keeps happening over and over again. The following is a list of the most common reasons love addicts keep falling into this trap.

- **Reminders of our first love:**
  - Most people are attracted to people who remind them of their first love. If a person's first love was an absent or emotionally unavailable parent, then he or she tends to be attracted to unavailable people, and these are the only people they pursue. This is done out of habit, despite the pain it will cause later on.

- **Looking for the happy ending:**
  - Many love addicts are not only attracted to unavailable people, they choose them as partners in order to recreate the past and change the ending. They often become obsessed trying to gain, through their current partner, the love they never got as a child. They do this unconsciously over and over again. It is a form of insanity. It is their inner child forcing his or her will on them despite the painful consequences. (See Recovery section for more about the inner child.)

- **Miscalculations:**
  - Many love addicts do not choose an unavailable person. They just fall in love before they find out the person is unavailable. Then, out of stubbornness, and because they have become so dependent, they refuse to give up and move on.

- **Unrequited love:**
  - Some love addicts can only fall in love with the person of their dreams. Since no such person really exists, they project their fantasies onto someone and then see

in that person only what they want to see. These completely unavailable people are a good target for this kind of projection because the love addict never really gets to know them. They are always who the love addict wants them to be. Love addicts, who are also addicted to fantasizing, are drawn to the phenomenon of unrequited love.

- **Excitement:**
  - Chasing after someone who is unavailable can be exciting. It can really get the adrenalin going, not to mention the libido. Romance addicts often go after unavailable people because they are addicted to the chase.

- **Unconscious fear of intimacy:**
  - While love addicts consciously obsess about love, they often have an underlying fear of intimacy. (This will be discussed more fully in Section VII.) Choosing to fall in love with someone who is unavailable (to one degree or another) is one way to avoid facing this fear.

BECOMING DEPENDENT ON AN ABUSIVE PARTNER

God grant me the serenity...to change the things I can...

The Serenity Prayer

Many love addicts find themselves drawn into abusive relationships and do not understand why. The following is a list of the most common conscious and unconscious reasons love addicts fall into this trap.

- **Love is blind:**

  – Most love addicts fall in love or get married before they find out their partner is abusive. The abusive partner keeps this hidden until the trap is sprung. After the abuse starts, these love addicts continue to love their abuser. They tell themselves that they are just taking the good with the bad.

- **Dependency on the relationship:**

  – Other love addicts don't love their abuser, but they are dependent on the relationship, and they would rather suffer physical pain than endure the emotional pain of breaking up. They cannot tolerate separation anxiety.

- **Low self-esteem:**

  – Some love addicts have such low self-esteem that they don't think they deserve any better. So they just stick with it. They think this is better than nothing.

- **Abusive parents:**

  – Some love addicts had an abusive parent so this abuse is not out of the ordinary for them. It is seen as the norm. It may even be equated with love. An abusive parent can also be loving, so battered children grow up confusing love with abuse. This confusion becomes a distorted value which influences them as adults.

- **Neighborhood norm:**

  – To some love addicts abuse may seem ordinary because all of their friends are being abused as well. In some neighborhoods domestic violence is the norm. It may seem futile to try and change the status quo.

- **It's my fault:**

  – Some love addicts blame themselves rather than their partner. They are sure it is their own fault—that they did something to provoke their partner. Sometimes they even think they deserve the abuse. They keep trying to change themselves so it won't happen anymore.

- **Gullibility:**
  - Some love addicts are gullible and don't learn from the past. They believe their partner when he or she says the abuse will never happen again. Like children, they cling to the fantasy that this person will change.

- **Sympathy:**
  - Many love addicts feel sorry for their partner when he or she asks for forgiveness. They know their partner is sick so they decide to take care of him or her rather than end the relationship. Caretakers are used to putting the needs of others before their own. This is misguided compassion.

- **Loyalty:**
  - When some love addicts make a commitment they feel they must be loyal no matter what—that they have no right to change their mind. They feel guilty if they reject someone, even if that someone is abusing them. This is misguided loyalty.

- **Projecting one's fear of abandonment:**
  - Some love addicts project their fear of abandonment onto their partners. They are so afraid of being rejected themselves that they become overly empathetic. They feel their partner will suffer from the rejection and they cannot bear to see someone else suffer, even someone who hurts them.

- **Fear of revenge:**
  - Many love addicts are terrified of leaving an abusive partner because they fear revenge or because they are financially dependent on this person.

- **Martyr's complex:**

  – Some love addicts have a martyr's complex. They feel superior when they suffer in the name of love. They wear abuse like a badge of courage. In a twisted sort of way this actually elevates their self-esteem. Christians especially fall into this trap. They think that because Christ died on the cross for the sins of mankind that they should die on the cross for the sins of their partner. They should not. They are not Christ. Some Christians read in the Bible that "love bears all things" and they think that this includes abuse. I don't think it does. Non-Christians fall into this trap also. They listen to the song "Stand by your man," and they think it is romantic to stick with a relationship no matter what.

- **Self-pity:**

  – Some love addicts let people abuse them because they like feeling sorry for themselves. They like licking their own wounds. Their self-esteem is so low that they substitute self-pity for self-love. Then they become dependent on the self-pity and allow, or even promote, abuse to get a fix.

- **Making up:**

  – Some love addicts don't like being abused, but they like making up. For instance, when their partner is begging for forgiveness they feel superior and in control. They like the attention. They like the flowers and apologies, so they talk themselves into believing that these gestures of remorse actually make up for the abuse.

- **Negative attention:**

  – Many love addicts are so starved for attention that even negative attention will do. They might tell themselves that if he didn't love me so much he wouldn't be so angry. This is twisted thinking and can lead to trouble.

- **Sexual stimulation:**
  - Some love addicts find some aspects of abuse sexually stimulating, so they endure the pain to get the pleasure that follows.

Warning

If having an abusive partner is a pattern, love addicts may have to face the fact that they have become addicted to the abuse—not to their partners. The phenomenon of pain followed by pleasure can be especially addictive. One actually starts to believe that the only way to find pleasure is to suffer first.

DUAL AND SUBSIDIARY ADDICTIONS

The content of the addiction, whether it be an ingestive addiction or an activity addiction…is an attempt at an intimate relationship.

JOHN BRADSHAW
in *Healing the Shame that Binds You*

Craig Nakken, in his book *The Addictive Personality: Roots, Rituals, and Recovery*, presents a strong case for the existence of a personality type underlying all addictions. He explains that the emergence of this personality begins as an escape from emotional pain and then takes on a life of its own as certain chosen rituals take form and become routinely acted out. This means that someone with an addictive personality can become dependent on more than one substance or experience.

Whether one believes in the addictive personality or not, it is well documented that addictions often come in clusters. Many alcoholics are also addicted to drugs. Workaholics are known for their obsessive spending. The combinations of various addictions are endless.

Love addicts have a wide range of subsidiary or dual-addictions. Hand in hand with their addiction to love can go an addiction to alcohol, drugs, eating, gambling, working, spending, or sex.

Those love addicts who are *dual-addicted* have developed other dependencies right along with their obsessions with regard to relationships. These other addictions are unrelated to their addiction to love and have a life of their own.

Most love addicts, however, have *subsidiary* or *potential* addictions. That is, their other obsessions only appear when they are having problems with relationships. For instance, some love addicts stop eating when they fall in love and become anorexic, especially if the person they are addicted to likes a slender partner; or they stop eating when a relationship ends because they are depressed. Other love addicts *over*eat compulsively when things go wrong in their relationship to numb the pain. I have also known love addicts who start drinking or using drugs because their partner is an alcoholic or drug addict, or they may be trying to escape the pain of an unhealthy relationship. Then there are the love addicts who shop compulsively to distract themselves from the pain of a deteriorating relationship or because they are angry at their partner and want to spend all of his or her money. Some love addicts will become workaholics to support their partners or to numb the pain of their addictive relationship.

The danger of subsidiary addictions is that they don't always stay that way. They have a tendency to progress, even if they come and go, and eventually they can reach the stage of being out of control.

OBSESSIONS THAT GO UNDERGROUND

Erotic love swears...they will love each other forever.

SØREN KIERKEGAARD in *Works of Love*

Some obsessions are like streams that go underground for awhile only to resurface later. These obsessions are perceived by love addicts as their undying love for a soul-mate. Sometimes these obsessions are the remnants of a love affair that has been cut short by death, divorce, abandonment, or other circumstances. At other times, the obsession is the by-product of unrequited, or forbidden love that has never been consummated. Whatever the circumstances, this type of passionate obsession always feels like a flame of desire that never goes out.

There are several unconscious motivations for obsessing on and off about the same person over the years. Sometimes it becomes the love addict's way of meeting his or her need for romantic stimulation in between relationships. In other words, if there is no available person to fantasize about, love addicts will reach back into the past and resurrect fantasies about the one who got away—the lost, forbidden, or unrequited love. This masks the love addict's fear of being single or alone.

Love addicts will also resurrect fantasies about an old love to ease the pain of an unhappy relationship. The old obsession provides a means of distracting the love addict from depression, fear and anger. It also allows them to avoid facing the reality of their current situation and delay making a decision about ending it.

Obsessions that go underground are insidious. Sometimes they are impossible to extricate. This is because they stem from an archetypal image—in this case the unconscious and

universal yearning to recapture what was lost, or to be reunited with someone. We see this dramatized time and time again
in romance novels. When I was growing up my favorite book
was about a woman who waited twenty years for her lover to
return from the Crusades.

HURTING OTHERS

The devil made me do it.

FLIP WILSON

Love addicts are emotionally immature and find it easy to see
their needs of the moment as a life or death struggle. When
caught up in their obsession, they become very self-absorbed.
In this state of mind they are unable to divide their time
between all the people who want or need their attention.

How does this self-absorption affect the love addict's family, co-workers, employers, or friends? Well, usually these people get neglected, abandoned, or abused. Love addicts stop
showing up for family functions. They don't spend any time
with their friends. They call in sick at work and lash out at
people they care about.

Children are especially affected by the self-absorption of
love addicts. In many cases love addicts have children to fulfill unmet emotional needs, and then they quickly abandon or
neglect their children when they find out that parenthood
does not take away their loneliness or hunger for love. Then
these love addicts will pursue an addictive relationship, hoping this will fix them, and the children just get in the way. The
result is more neglect and abandonment. I have known love
addicts who left their children in cars for hours so they could
go into a bar to meet a man. One woman I knew even left her
son standing out in the rain while she was inside the house
with her lover who didn't want the child around. This woman

(Jane) shared with me how she stood looking out the window watching her son Peter. She said she felt paralyzed, unable to put her addiction aside to take care of her son. Eventually, Peter knocked on the door, and with tears in his eyes, he asked to come in. Jane said, "I'll be out in a minute." An hour later she still hadn't come out.

CRIMES OF THE HEART

Is it, in Heav'n, a crime to love too well?

ALEXANDER POPE in *Elegy to the Memory of an Unfortunate Lady*

As addiction to love progresses into the later stages, some love addicts will experience a form of temporary insanity. By this I mean that an abnormal state of mind takes over some love addicts, and they become powerless over their own behavior. It is in this altered state of consciousness that love addicts put everything on the line in the name of love. Some love addicts in this condition will even break the law despite all the risks involved.

Crimes of the heart are not all the same. Sometimes they are just the result of misguided loyalty, the obsessive need to stand by your loved one no matter what the cost. In other words, some love addicts will get talked into being an accomplice to a crime. They lack the ability to say "no" to their partner, or to set limits on what they will do to keep the relationship going. Being an accomplice can mean anything from driving the car in an armed robbery to harboring a fugitive. It might also mean perjury. These acts are usually not done without a great deal of remorse. I am not talking about Bonnie and Clyde here. Most love addicts agonize over their decision to become involved in situations that are dangerous and against the law. They have a healthy sense of right or wrong, but regardless of their fears or misgivings they become powerless over their need to hold on to their partner. They are dependent people, and they give new meaning to the word sacrifice.

Love addicts, who are also caretakers, will sometimes commit crimes to make money, which they then use to take care of their partner. Love addicts who are unable to hold down a full time job are particularly susceptible to this temptation. They may become prostitutes or drug dealers in order to support their partner. However, even employed love addicts have been known to steal money to meet the desires, or imagined needs, of the person they are addicted to. Perhaps they are involved with a drug addict and feel responsible for supporting his or her cocaine addiction. When love addicts don't make enough money to keep their partners supplied, they embezzle money. In 1985, the head of the Housing Authority in a well-known West Coast city resigned because she was suspected of pocketing money to support her husband's drug habit. Needless to say her career was ruined.

The mantra of the love addict/caretaker is, "If I take care of you will you love me," and once a relationship has been established using this as the guiding principle, love addicts will go to any length to meet their end of the bargain. They will risk their safety and freedom to take care of someone they have become enmeshed with and emotionally dependent on. Once again, most love addicts know what they are doing is wrong, or dangerous; still, they risk everything because they are blinded by their addiction.

Many crimes of the heart involve violence. Sometimes this happens when love addicts become overwhelmed by their abnormal jealousy and possessiveness—usually when the relationship is breaking up and they become unable to control themselves. In a state of temporary insanity some love addicts try to take control of the situation by becoming violent. They think, "If I can't have you no one can." This is the scenario we see in the movie "Fatal Attraction." In real life we see this illustrated in the case of Jean Harris who was convicted of killing Dr. Tarnover in upstate New York. In another recent case, a man in Northern California killed his estranged wife because he felt he could not live without her. Then he took his young daughter to the Golden Gate Bridge and threw her over the side. Within seconds he had jumped in after her.

Still another interesting example of violence in an addictive relationship is illustrated by the story of a woman I once saw once on the Oprah Winfrey show. She was a love addict trying to liberate herself from an abusive relationship. She left her partner and he began to harass her (threatening phone calls, slashed tires, etc.). She called the police and got no help. She got a restraining order and her former lover ignored it. In desperation she bought a gun to protect herself. Then, the next time her partner showed up to harass her, she became overwhelmed by her fear and shot him. Like others in a similar situation, this woman was not protected by the law, and she went to jail. (There are strict legal guidelines for self-defense, and many people who try to protect themselves from an abusive partner are convicted of a crime.) If you doubt that this woman was a love addict, just because she was trying to get out of the relationship, let me add that while she was out on bail for shooting this man she took him into her home and cared for him as he recuperated from the gunshot wounds she had inflicted.

The most serious crimes connected to addictive relationships involve children. Some love addicts are convicted of child endangerment because of their addiction. A few years ago I watched a woman on a well-known talk show try to explain why she left her children clinging to a fence on a busy freeway. She was trying to make the audience understand that her boyfriend had insisted that she abandon her children and she felt powerless to disobey him.

Even more astounding are the cases of love addicts who stand by while their children are abused or even murdered by their partner. This sounds horrendous and unbelievable. How can this happen? Well, once again, many love addicts feel *powerless* over their need to hold onto a relationship no matter what the cost. In such cases, obsession and dependency have taken their toll. Either out of misguided loyalty, or to avoid separation anxiety (withdrawal), some love addicts stand by in a state of suspended animation while their children are abused; or they ignore the signs that abuse has occurred, hoping that the problem will go away if they bury their heads in the sand. This is the darkest side of addiction to love—the inability of some love addicts to even protect their children from an abusive partner because of their unhealthy dependency.

While most love addicts will not end up breaking the law in the name of love, the *hungry heart* should not be underestimated. Addiction to love is insidious and progressive; anything can happen if recovery is not initiated. When a crime *is* committed because of obsession and dependency, love addicts pay a heavy price. Sometimes they must spend all or some of their lives in prison. They must also live with the guilt they feel for subjecting themselves and others to their temporary insanity. Even if they are not caught, love addicts have to live with the remorse and the loss of self-esteem that results from being powerless over an addiction. To say the least, their lives are affected in a dramatic and negative way.

III.

CONTRIBUTING FACTORS THAT INFLUENCE POTENTIAL LOVE ADDICTS

From the bondage of sorrow, the captives dream dreams.

JIM MANLEY in *Spirit*

CONTRIBUTING FACTORS

A person is not going to become a love addict unless he or she has low self-esteem, an excessive hunger for love, and a tremendous fear of abandonment. These are the primary motivating factors. However, there are some other contributing factors as well, and while they play a lesser role in the addiction process, they are worth mentioning.

LOVE SONGS AND MYTHS ABOUT ROMANTIC LOVE

One of these contributing factors is the perpetuation by the media of distorted notions about romantic love. By "media" I mean romantic novels, movies, television shows, and music. Of course, the biggest culprit when it comes to spreading misconceptions about romance is the love song. It is from listening to love songs over and over again that we are saturated with the message that *life is not worth living without romantic love*, and that we are *nobody until somebody loves us*. Love songs also tell us that love is an *endless aching need* and that it is all right to *go crazy* when we fall in love. As long as I can remember I have been hearing that love is *magic*, that the first time you meet someone the *sun should rise in their eyes,* and that it is all right to *dream your life away.*

Love songs also reinforce the idea that it is all right to suffer for love. I have heard songs that say in essence *do what you want to me but don't let me be lonely.* There is also a multitude of songs about *heartache* and *standing by your partner* even if your partner is a liar and a cheat. Other songs glorify *needing to be needed* in conjunction with suffering in the name of love. They repeat the same message—as long as I am *needed,* I will be *true* and *hang in there no matter what.*

My favorite songs are about the people who will do *anything* to lure a loved into their lives and *anything* to hold on to them. (In case you've missed my point, these songs are about controlling, not loving.)

Of course, love songs don't always give the wrong messages. After all, I have heard some great lyrics about *enough is enough* or *sometimes love just ain't enough.* Still, while many love songs are just harmless melodies about how *hard it is to break up,* others perpetuate serious misconceptions or myths about romantic love. They reinforce the erroneous ideas that:

- Love happens overnight.

- Falling in love is like drinking a magic potion and you should allow yourself to be drawn into this experience despite the consequences. (In other words it is all right to be irresponsible when it comes to love.)

- Romantic love is the most important experience in life; it is the *only* fulfilling experience worth having; and other forms of love (platonic, familial, brotherly, spiritual, etc.) are worthless substitutes.

- It is all right to do anything in the name of love. (All's fair in love and war.)

- It is romantic to suffer (or even die) for the sake of love.

SUGGESTIONS

- Put romantic love into perspective. Don't let the poets tell you how to think about love. Love is not something you are powerless over. It is not the most important experience in life. It is not all right to do anything in the name of love, and it is not romantic to suffer.

ROLE STRUCTURING

women only

Unfortunately, in almost every society known to "man," women are ultimately taught that their primary identity is linked to their relationship with a man, while men are taught that their primary identity is linked to their work. As a result, most women tend to feel deprived or devalued when there is no man in their lives. Of course, potential love addicts are especially susceptible to this notion, and (as usual) take it one step further. Not only do they have misgivings about being single, this role horrifies them. It is a fate worse than death.

SUGGESTIONS

- Consider creating your own personal values regarding the importance of being in an intimate relationship. (Don't think like a needy, addictive person.)

- Try not to be influenced by the hidden messages of the media and literature. Laugh at them, ignore them, or get angry and protest them, but don't buy into them.

- Read *Why Do I Think I'm Nothing Without a Man*, by Penelope Russianoff.

INADEQUATE ROLE MODELS

Not only are children who have had a dysfunctional childhood deprived of love and guidance, they are given poor examples to follow. Therefore, a love addict with an emotionally unhealthy parent will often see addictive (or neurotic) behavior as normal. This makes it especially difficult to recognize and change obsessive behavior—but not impossible.

SUGGESTIONS

- Don't follow the example set by your parents if you recognize their behavior as being obsessive, addictive, or unhealthy in terms of today's standards. For instance, you don't have to be a martyr just because your mother was.

- For those who now recognize their parents as poor or inadequate role models, consider beginning a process of "cutting loose." Find new role-models, and begin forming your own "adult" values. Also, learn to replace inappropriate behavior, based on old ideas, with healthy behavior based on your newly formed values.

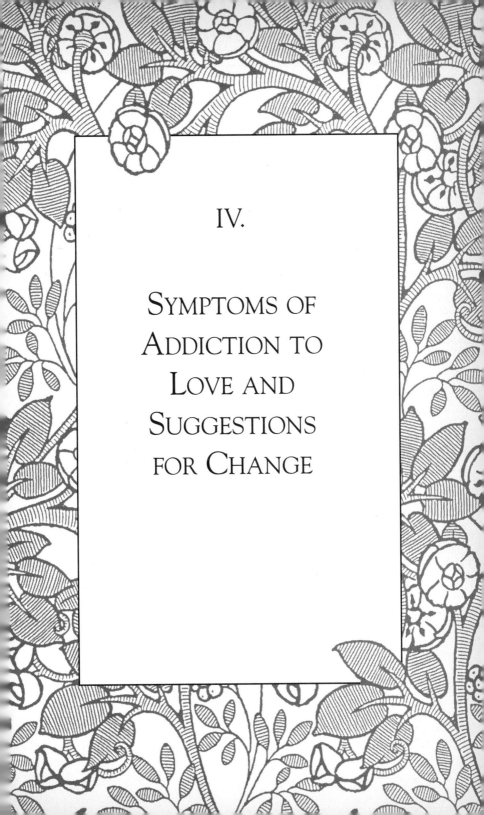

IV.

Symptoms of Addiction to Love and Suggestions for Change

Alas, of all the enemies, habit is perhaps the most cunning, and it is cunning enough never to let itself be seen, for he who sees the habit is saved from the habit.

SØREN KIERKEGAARD in *Works of Love*

LOVE AT FIRST SIGHT

Love addicts have many needs; one of the most compelling is the need to connect with someone. This is more than a healthy attachment hunger. This need is usually overwhelming, and most love addicts feel powerless to control it.

Because of this inner compulsion love addicts are impatient to bond with someone before they really get a chance to know him or her. I call this phenomenon "love at first sight" or premature bonding.

Love at first sight creates problems for love addicts. It either overwhelms the people they fall in love with (pushing them away) or it makes it difficult for love addicts to pull out of a relationship even when they find out they have fallen in love with the wrong person.

SUGGESTIONS

- Beware of your neediness and take your time when getting to know someone.

- Don't always lead with your heart or let your attraction to someone become more powerful than your common sense.

- Take measures to modify your obsessive behavior even if an infatuation is blossoming. Maintain the lifestyle you had before you met this person.

- Make note of the types of people you are attracted to. If the same kind of person always triggers your addictive tendencies (and the result has always been disastrous), then stay away from this type—even if you think you are in love.

- Don't confuse lust or attraction with love. There is no such experience as love at first sight. Love is the by-product of a healthy relationship.

EXCESSIVE FANTASIZING

For the love addict, excessive fantasizing plays a prominent role throughout the whole addiction process. When they first fall in love, love addicts trigger their addiction with fantasies about the loved one. Later, when their addiction takes off, it is characterized by an obsessive preoccupation with the loved one, or a constant repetition of thoughts (fantasies) about the new lover. When the relationship begins to deteriorate, the love addict avoids facing the reality of the situation by day-dreaming about "how it was," or "how it is going to be when things get better." Even after love addicts have separated from a partner, they often keep the addiction alive by dreaming of being reunited. Fantasizing, it seems, carries the addiction forth. It keeps the infatuation, preoccupation, and obsession alive.

Since fantasizing about relationships is second nature to most people, it is important to know when it is normal and when it becomes symptomatic of an addiction. Here are some guidelines.

- How much time do you spend fantasizing? Too much time?

- Is it hard to stop fantasizing once you have started?

- Is it impossible to stop fantasizing once you have started?

- Does fantasizing take priority over other activities? Do you stay home all the time to dream about your loved one rather than go out and have fun?

- Does fantasizing take priority over your responsibilities? Do you put aside your housework to lie in bed and fantasize? Do you stay home from work?

- Do you daydream when it is dangerous to do so (such as when you are driving a car or operating machinery)?

- Does fantasizing take priority over your family and friends? Do you brush aside your children to go off by yourself and daydream? Do you snap at people who interrupt your fantasies?

- Do your fantasies become a substitute for reality? Do you settle for a fantasy life rather than make changes in your circumstances?

- Do you empower your fantasies? Do they become expectations or dreams that have to come true?

SUGGESTIONS

- Answer the above questions. Be honest. If you answer yes to more than a few, you probably fantasize too much. You may even be addicted to fantasizing.

- If you fantasize excessively, recognize this and look at the motives behind it.

- Don't let excessive fantasizing take priority over other activities.

- Don't distort or try to escape the reality of your life by fantasizing.

- Discipline yourself when you are alone. When you start drifting off into a fantasy, stop yourself or put a time limit on it. (This is called "thought stopping.")

- If you tend to fantasize obsessively, structure your time more carefully. Find constructive things to do. When it is time to relax, read or watch television rather than drift off into a fantasy.

- Don't let childhood fantasies guide your selection of a partner. Determine what your needs are as an adult. Consider your age, standards, taste, spiritual values, environment, and so on, but not your childhood romantic fantasies.

- Don't let your fantasies become expectations or dreams that have to come true. Be flexible about what makes you happy.

- When you are facing reality on a daily basis and "living in the moment," begin thinking about improvements that can be made in yourself and changes that can be made in your situation. Use dreaming as a way to make realistic and mature plans for your life. Dreams are constructive if they are used as a blueprint for working toward realistic success and happiness.

THE NEED TO CREATE DRAMA
AND EXCITEMENT

Because love addicts are so captivated by romance (it seems like the solution to all their problems), they always feel the urge to see all the events of their lives as dramatic episodes in some great "soap opera." Furthermore, because love addicts equate drama and excitement with romance, they always feel an unconscious urge (compulsion) to try and create drama. This produces a "high" akin to the "rush" experienced by the drug addict.

There are several ways in which love addicts typically try to create drama. Sometimes they stir up trouble in order to create excitement. For example, love addicts are very good at picking fights when their relationship seems boring. They are also very good at trying to turn an ordinary event into an extra-ordinary experience (just for the excitement). By this I mean that love addicts are not only capable of picking a fight, they will also try to turn an argument into a war (blow it out of proportion) just because this brings an adrenaline rush.

Love addicts also like to create drama in their minds by trying to "read between the lines" and interpret other people's actions: "She smiled at me, it must mean she loves me; she didn't smile at me, it must mean she hates me." Or they will try to read other people's minds and make assumptions not based on facts: "I just know he really loves me no matter what he says; I just know he really hates me no matter what he says." Or they will imagine that their romantic dreams have come true long before there is any evidence to back that up that assumption. This is our third date—I know he is going to ask me to marry him. In other words, love addicts tend to see reality only in terms of their own needs. This can mean they are seeing what is not really there or they are misreading the facts.

Of course, creating drama may make ordinary experiences more exciting, but it also means that unpleasant experiences are over-dramatized and taken all too seriously. This sets the love addict up for disappointment which can lead to unnecessary emotional pain (which in turn triggers the love addict's fears and obsessive behavior). Furthermore, while the need to create drama and excitement stems from the need of love addicts to have access to the euphoric "high" of romance, it never occurs to them that they might need more excitement than is healthy. Also, it is very difficult for them to accept that a relationship is often a mixture of highs and lows—or less than a Shakespearean play. This is one of the reasons love addicts never have healthy relationships. They walk away from nice people because they are not feeling excited every minute of the day (they call this boredom); and they tend to be attracted to relationships that are exciting all the time, even if that drama comes from chaos, repetitive fighting, or obsessive behavior. I cannot tell you how many times my students have said to me "I don't think I am in love because I just don't feel that thrill all the time—that excitement and drama." This euphoria is what love addicts are looking for and they balk at any relationship that does not deliver a constant supply.

SUGGESTIONS

- Read about this phenomenon. (For women, I suggest *The Agony of It All: The Drive for Drama and Excitement in Women's Lives* by Joy Davidson.)

- Look honestly at your need to create drama.

- Ask yourself why you might be unconsciously trying to create drama.

  - Did you grow up fantasizing about romantic drama as an escape from painful feelings? Are you now, without realizing it, trying to live out your dreams?

  - Do you frequently read romantic novels that portray love as constantly exciting, therefore reinforcing your need for a continuing supply of drama in your relationship?

  - Did you grow up in a home where negative drama (chaos) was the norm? If so, are you constantly trying to re-live childhood experiences or cling to the familiarity of that kind of negative form of excitement?

- Do you like drama because you have never learned to appreciate or value the absence of excitement?
- Are you hooked on the stimulus of drama because you are so needy (starved for attention)?

• Consider learning how to appreciate the ordinary experiences of life. Learn to value the absence of excitement—to see it as a resting place in the relationship.

• Try to identify the ways in which you over-dramatize events or see drama where it really doesn't exist. Make a list.

• Try to observe yourself and then write about the times you catch yourself creating drama by picking a fight, exaggerating ordinary events, or fantasizing excessively. You might notice that there is a connection between your need to control and your habit of creating drama. Love addicts like to produce the show, direct it, and write the script.

• Once you know what to watch out for, try to stop creating drama. Consider evaluating events more realistically. It might also help to take yourself, and your relationship, less seriously.

• Learn how to stop yourself in the middle of the second act. Eventually you will learn how to cancel the show before it goes on.

EXAGGERATED FEARS IN RELATIONSHIPS

Because love addicts are needy and have fears left over from childhood, they are terrified of loneliness, abandonment, rejection and being deprived of love.

- They feel life is not worth living without romantic love or an intimate relationship.

- They are terrified of being alone.

- They are suicidal when relationships break up.

- They cling too long to unhealthy relationships rather than face their fears.

- When they are in an addictive relationship, they are terrified of "rocking the boat." They fear the relationship might end.

- They feel as if they can't survive as an individual.

- They have an exaggerated level of anxiety about the progress of their relationship. This is expressed as:
  – Chronic nervousness and the inability to concentrate on other things.
  – Extreme impatience—the need to rush things along as a validation that there is going to be a happy ending.
  – An over-reaction to the least setback in the relationship.

SUGGESTIONS

- Look at your fears and how they affect your life.

- Look at your history of abandonment and rejection.

- Try to face your fears.

- Try not to let your fears rule your life. You do not have to give in to your fears.

- Re-evaluate your attitude about being alone. Don't confuse solitude with loneliness, or being in a relationship with security.

- Let relationships take their natural course. Don't think that each time you meet someone it will be the last chance you have.

- Develop a spiritual program to help abate your fears and work on building up your self-esteem.

ABNORMAL JEALOUSY

Because love addicts are insecure and afraid, they are abnormally jealous or possessive. They do not love their partners. They take them hostage.

- They are always anxious when their partner is not present.

- They worry constantly about what their partner is doing when he or she is not in sight.

- They give their partner the third-degree all the time.

In assessing the term "abnormal" consider:

- How much time do you spend worrying? Is it excessive?

- What is your level of anxiety? Is it overwhelming?

- What things do you do because of jealousy? (Do you drive by your lover's house at 3:00 in the morning to see if he or she is home?)

SUGGESTIONS

- Find a partner that is trustworthy.

- Even if you feel jealous, don't act on it and become possessive. Don't let it rule your life.

- Work on building up your self-esteem and developing a

healthy relationship with yourself to prevent insecurity that leads to abnormal jealousy.

DYSFUNCTIONAL EMOTIONS

Most love addicts are confused and overwhelmed by their emotions because of painful childhood experiences. As a result:

- They are afraid of expressing their anger with someone they love (especially someone they are addicted to). They think their anger has the power to drive people away. They associate expressing anger with rejection and abandonment.

- They experience overwhelming and painful feelings that seem unrelated to the circumstances of their present life (free-floating anxiety, old feelings left over from childhood, etc.).

- They tend to have polarized feelings (all or nothing).
  - agony or ecstasy
  - euphoria or depression
  - hyper-vigilance or complacency
  - love or hate
  - fear or bravado
  - low self-esteem or egomania
  - rage or numbness

- They feel an overwhelming need to control their emotions especially when it comes to feelings that might force them to see the truth about their addictive relationships.
  - They try to substitute one emotion for another or to feel a less threatening emotion when another would

be more appropriate. (They feel guilty when they
should feel angry.)

 – They tend to deny painful feelings (to themselves and
  to others).

 – They suppress or bury painful feelings rather than feel
  them directly. They can be very stoic.

 – They often anesthetize painful feelings with drugs,
  alcohol, food, or fantasies about romantic love.

SUGGESTIONS

• Go for help. Share your confusion with others who
 understand your situation.

• Reflect on your childhood experiences and consider
 how you may have been steered in the wrong direction
 with regard to your feelings.

 – Did your parents make you feel ashamed of your feelings?

 – Did they criticize you for your honest emotional reaction to situations?

 – Did your parents often say to you, "You shouldn't feel
  that way," or "Nice children don't react that way."?

 – When it comes to expressing feelings appropriately,
  were your parents good role models?

• Do some reading on the subject. Accept the fact that
 you are operating with outdated information and need
 to know how healthy people respond to their feelings.

• Learn how to identify the fears that underlie such emotions as anger and depression. (Many feelings are just a
 reaction to our hidden fears.)

• Always ask yourself if you are experiencing emotions
 that are appropriate to the situation. Do they make
 sense or are they just habitual responses left over from

childhood? For example, if your partner has been dishonest and you immediately feel guilty, have the courage to realize that this reaction is not appropriate. The more appropriate response is to get angry.

• Don't numb yourself with substances like sugar, alcohol or drugs. Feel your feelings so that they will motivate you to face the truth about your addiction.

• Accept your feelings without making value judgments. For instance, anger is not bad. It can motivate you to change negative conditions in your life. How you handle the anger might be right or wrong, but the feeling itself is not.

• Learn how to channel feelings appropriately. Talk about them openly and honestly. Write about them as much as you can.

• Learn how to express anger in a healthy way.
  – Directed at the person you are angry with:
    Letters
    Confrontation
  – Alone:
    Exercise
    Painting
    Beating a pillow
    Scream therapy
  – With a third party:
    In therapy
    Through role-playing
    With a friend
    In a support group

• Remember, learning how to deal with your feelings is a slow process. Be patient and loving with yourself.

WEAK PERSONALITY BOUNDARIES

Personality boundaries are like a fence around a house. The fence acts as a property line giving the person in the house a sense of where his or her space ends and someone else's begins. The fence can also act as a protective barrier keeping intruders out. At the same time, the owner of the property can put a gate in the fence allowing friendly people to come in. Or the owner of the property can go through the gate to explore other people's property. However, they always go back home where they live. They never stay in someone else's space.

Most love addicts have weak personality boundaries because of their low self-esteem. As a result they become too enmeshed with their partners and lose their sense of individuality. In other words, they don't know where their needs, wants, emotions, and values leave off and their partner's begins. If their partner is happy they are happy. If their partner is sad they are sad. If their partner hates someone they hate someone. If their partner votes for a particular candidate they vote for the same candidate. Love addicts often completely abandon themselves and become either an imitation of their partner (when they look into the mirror they see their partner instead of themselves) or who their partner wants them to be.

When love addicts do have a sense of their own personality—who they are as opposed to who their partner is—they often can't protect their integrity. They can't say "no" or set limits. They can't stand up for themselves and keep their partner from crashing over their boundaries. They can't say "What you see is what you get" or "Don't make me over." They can't say "I will not do that." In other words, they can't keep from being controlled by their partners. (These love addicts will appear to others as "door mats.")

SUGGESTIONS

- Define yourself. Do some thinking and writing about who you are. What do you believe in? What is your style? What do you like? What don't you like? What kind of personality do you have? Be specific!

- Reveal who you are to others (be yourself). Don't hold back or try to be someone else just to please your partner.

- Put some space between you and others—a healthy amount—not too much and not too little.

- Be your own champion and protect yourself from people who want to change you into another person. Say "no" to people who want you to turn yourself inside out to please them. Say "no" to people who want you to do something you do not want to do. Build a fence around yourself (not a wall) and only let people in who will not try to control you—people who like you just the way you are.

HIGH LEVEL OF TOLERANCE FOR SUFFERING IN RELATIONSHIPS

Many love addicts (especially relationship addicts) have a very high tolerance for chronic neglect and abuse because:

- They can't stand the pain of breaking up (separation anxiety or withdrawal). This is sort of like living with a backache to avoid painful surgery.

- Having suffered a lot as a child (when they were powerless to change the situation) suffering has become familiar and therefore comfortable.

SUGGESTIONS

- Never accept or rationalize abuse. You deserve better.

- Don't settle for neglect as an alternative to ending an addictive relationship. If your partner consistently neglects you, face this and work toward making changes.

- Look at the possibility that you might have become addicted to the pain. (See *Addiction and Grace* by Gerald May.)

ACCEPTING DISHONESTY

For the same reasons that love addicts are willing to suffer for love, they are also willing to accept dishonesty in a relationship.

Note that dishonesty includes cheating, defrauding, deceiving, lying, and the omission of information crucial to maintaining the integrity of the relationship. For the love addict accepting dishonesty is part of a complex denial system which includes:

- Ignoring obvious inconsistencies in a partner's behavior.

- Ignoring nonsensical explanations of how a partner spends his or her time.

- Ignoring the omission of crucial information.

- Ignoring unusual exhibitions of guilt shown through a partner's body language.

- Not asking questions or checking out information even if it sounds "fishy."

- Trying desperately not to be suspicious (despite their fears).

When dishonesty is too obvious to ignore, love addicts defend their partners by telling themselves that:

- He didn't mean to do it.

- She was desperate.

- He loved me too much to tell me the truth. (He didn't want to hurt my feelings.)

- She won't do it again.

- I pushed him into doing it. It's my fault.

- She didn't have a good role model as a child, so she doesn't know any better.

- He will change.

- This is the first time she's done this in a long time.

- All people are a little dishonest, they are only human.

- Half-truths are not lies. Half-truths don't count.

- I must have heard him wrong.

Even when dishonesty is not rationalized, love addicts will do anything to avoid confronting their partner's dishonesty. They will make one or more of the following excuses:

- There is nothing I can do about it.

- I don't know them well enough to have a confrontation.

- It is not up to me to point out their character defects.

- I can't prove it, so why bring it up.

- He will only deny it like he always does.

- She might be angry.

- He might not love me any more.

- She might leave me.

- I don't like to fight about these things.

- I just want to forget the whole thing.
- Now is not the time, I'll bring it up later. (Later never ever comes.)

SUGGESTIONS

- If you are in the habit of accepting or ignoring dishonesty as a tradeoff for holding on to someone, try to stop. Confront your partner.

- Confronting dishonesty in an ongoing relationship is important, but be warned. After years of game-playing, your partner may not want to change. If your partner does agree to change, remember that the habitual liar will not change overnight. Therefore, you must see him or her really take action before you get your hopes up. The dishonesty must end and he or she must get some help. You must also be vigilant and watch out for attempts to slide back into old patterns and games.

- Avoid relationships that are based on a lie (such as an affair with someone who is married).

- Determine early in a relationship whether or not your partner is honest and take a stand on this issue. Confront your partner if he or she lies; and end the relationship if the lies continue.

- Do not make excuses for dishonesty. Take into account a person's dishonesty with others (people often talk openly about this). Do not assume that you will avoid the same fate if you get involved. Realize that if a person is dishonest there is very little chance that he or she will change without a conscious effort. Understand that liars will not change out of love for you.

- Ask questions if you are suspicious. Check out information. Considering your history as a love addict, it is all right to be cautious. Up to now you have ignored your suspicions and buried your head in the sand. Now is the time to investigate if need be. This is not the same as giving the third degree to a trustworthy partner because you are jealous. (See earlier discussion about abnormal jealousy.)

- Be honest yourself, and then expect the same from your partner.

BEING RULED BY YOUR LIBIDO

If the love addict's fantasy of "living happily ever after" is associated exclusively with attachment and bonding, then he or she is not necessarily dominated by his or her sexual needs. The love addict will even do without sex rather than give up on a relationship. Indeed, some love addicts stay with partners who ignore them sexually. (Relationship addicts do this a lot.) However, if eroticism is part of the love addict's fantasy, he or she is apt to:

- Confuse lust with love.

- Become blinded by a sexual attraction to someone.

- Let passion take precedence over other more important aspects of the relationship such as companionship, commitment, friendship, honesty, communication, etc.

SUGGESTIONS

- Take the time to evaluate your sexual behavior.

- Don't let passion blind you to other important aspects of the relationship.

- If you are attracted to an unhealthy person, nip this in the bud. Don't spend a lot of time with someone just because they are sexually attractive. Also, try not to fantasize about this person.

- Read some material about sexual addiction. This phenomenon differs somewhat from addiction to love. (See *Out of the Shadows*, by Patrick Carnes.)

CONFUSING NEED WITH WANT

Because love addicts are hungry for love and acceptance, the reinforcing effects of their addictive relationship become a need not a want. It becomes a compulsion that can't be ignored. Therefore, romance, relationships, fantasies, etc. are all a life or death matter, not the icing on the cake.

SUGGESTIONS

- Sort out your needs from you wants. Be honest. Use your head, not your heart.

- If your wants are not good for you, try not to pursue them. Learn self-discipline.

THE COMPELLING NEED TO CONTROL

The beginning of love is to let those we love
be perfectly themselves, and not to twist them
to fit our own image.

THOMAS MERTON in *No Man is an Island*

Once they are in an addictive relationship, love addicts want to make their dreams come true, diminish their fear of loneliness and abandonment, and avoid losing their partner.

Controlling is how love addicts try to meet these needs. Most of the controlling techniques used in addictive relationships are passive-aggressive in nature (manipulative rather than direct demands for control). This is because:

- The love addict may be using management techniques learned during childhood when he or she was powerless to exert more direct forms of control.

- For female love addicts, passive-aggressive controlling techniques are part of their cultural legacy. Having lived for centuries with the burden of social powerlessness, women have learned how to manipulate as a way of gaining culturally accepted power within a relationship. (At one time this protected women and gave them some badly needed freedom, but today it is an outdated way for women to relate to men.)

- While love addicts have a strong need to control, they do not want to risk going too far and driving their partner away. Therefore, manipulation seems safer than outright attempts to control.

- Because passive-aggressive controlling techniques are usually harder to recognize and identify, they are easier to rationalize or deny. This makes them more tempting as methods of control.

To further illustrate the relationship between controlling and addiction to love, I have listed, on the following pages, some of the most common controlling techniques used by love addicts.

IMAGE MANAGEMENT

Image management is what love addicts do to control someone's impressions of them through what amounts to deceit and dishonesty, or just hiding who they really are. When they are just getting to know someone, love addicts who are image managers try to:

- Filter out information about themselves that may not look good.

- Tell outright lies about who they are or what they have done in the past.

- Tell too much about their "miserable existence" as a means of soliciting pity.

- Try to make an all out effort to promote their best side. This means spending a great deal of time and energy looking just right, saying the right things, and being in the right place at the right time. It means being inflexible and a perfectionist.

Once they get into a relationship, image managers:

- Try to become the person they think their lover wants them to be (no matter what the cost).

- Give their partner mixed signals. This is because love addicts vacillate between saying what they really mean and what their partner wants to hear. For example, love addicts may initially say "no" to their partner about something and then quickly change their mind if their partner has a negative reaction. Sometimes love addicts even volunteer to do something for their partner (as a way to score points) and then they get angry at their partner when it comes time to deliver.

Love addicts are almost always image managers. They rationalize this as a normal part of "getting their mate" or "putting their best foot forward," but actually their behavior is motivated by their need to control and the fear that they are unlovable. Therefore, the more insecure love addicts are, the more driven they are to protect, promote, or manage their image to insure the survival of their relationship or keep the attention of a lover. (Children who grow up in dysfunctional homes learn image management early because they are trying to hide the truth about their family. Later it becomes a habitual way of relating to people.)

SUGGESTIONS

- If you are an image manager, be more honest about who you are and learn how to be true to yourself. Do not lie or make yourself over just because you are desperate to get someone's attention. Instead, build up your self-esteem so you do not feel the need to hide behind an image or facade.

- Say what you mean and then stick to it. If you say "no," don't change your mind just to keep your partner happy. Don't offer to do things you really do not want to do, or to give people things you really do not want to give them.

NAGGING

Nagging is an attempt to wear someone down so they will give in to you, even if they don't want to. Love addicts love to nag (if it works), because it is a nonthreatening way to get what they want (need). They don't know how to communicate their needs in any other way or how to find a person who doesn't need to be nagged. Therefore, nagging becomes a habitual way to manage a partner rather than face the inadequacies of the relationship or work on improving themselves. (Nagging includes nonstop criticism and advice.)

SUGGESTIONS

- If nagging is your way of trying to control your partner, or the only way you can get your needs met, you might consider making changes.

- Begin by not giving in to the temptation to nag. State what you consider to be a reasonable request and then drop it. If you are ignored then discuss how this is undermining the relationship. If this communication

does not get results then consider ending the relationship.

- Avoid giving constant unsolicited advice. A suggestion
  now and then is more appropriate.

- Stop endless criticism. Offer constructive criticism once
  or twice and then let it go.

- Try to note early on in a relationship whether or not
  the person you are with has to be nagged before he or
  she will consider your needs. Look for unsolicited affection and consideration.

- Work on improving yourself, not nagging others to
  change. They are responsible for initiating their own
  self-improvement.

BEING HELPLESS

Acting helpless around a partner is another classic
passive-aggressive controlling technique. It projects the
unspoken message that "I can't survive without you." If this
works, a love addict will try it. Women especially like to rationalize this as being "feminine" or "stroking a man's ego." They
won't do anything alone, and they avoid all activities that suggest they can take care of themselves.

SUGGESTIONS

- If you are a person who likes the image of being "helpless," stop being totally dependent on your partner as a
  means of controlling him or her.

- However, don't confuse accepting support from your
  partner with acting helpless. The goal is to find a
  healthy balance between taking care of yourself and letting others help you.

PROJECTING GUILT

Often, when love addicts find themselves in a situation where their needs are not being met, they attempt to manipulate the situation by trying to make their partner feel guilty. They keep a long list of their partner's transgressions and don't hesitate to remind them of every mistake they ever made. Or they play the martyr when their partner is out of line, hoping this will stimulate remorse and change.

SUGGESTIONS

- Try to learn how to tell the difference between honestly pointing out the truth and trying to make your partner feel guilty as a controlling technique.

- Making your partner feel guilty may get short-term results, but it is still not an emotionally mature way to interact with someone, and in the long run it erodes a relationship. If your partner is constantly doing things which he or she should feel guilty about, then something is wrong with the relationship and changes should be made.

- Don't accept outrageous behavior just so you can use it later to make your partner feel guilty.

STIMULATING JEALOUSY

Because love addicts are so insecure, they need constant reassurance that a relationship is going strong. Stimulating their partner's jealousy is an attempt to capture this reassurance—to control it. It is also used as a way to keep one's partner on edge and anxious to please. Or sometimes it is used as a way to draw a partner back into a relationship when he or she seems to be straying. Of course this is often rationalized as an acceptable way to keep the relationship exciting, but it is really a controlling technique and has no place in a healthy relationship.

SUGGESTIONS

- If you are in the habit of trying to make your partner jealous, try to stop. Don't flirt with others outrageously just to get his or her attention.

- Consciously making your partner jealous may seem exhilarating and bring you badly needed reassurance, but the distress it causes them is really not fair. To one degree or another we are all a little possessive of the person we love, but provoking jealousy as a way of playing on this natural tendency is not what a healthy relationship is all about. If you need to make your partner jealous to feel loved, then work on your emotional neediness and give them a break.

FLATTERY

Flattery is fine if it is a genuine attempt to stroke your partner as part of your mutual support of each other. However, if it is just a way to "soften up your partner" it is another form of passive-aggressive controlling.

SUGGESTIONS

- If you like to flatter your partner for manipulative reasons, try to stop.

- Ask yourself if your partner is giving you strokes too. If not, then maybe you are monopolizing the giving of compliments in your relationship in order to take control. Talk about this and learn to give each other verbal support.

THE SILENT TREATMENT

The silent treatment is also part of the love addict's long list of passive-aggressive controlling techniques. It is used to get a partner's attention or to make him or her feel guilty. Or it can be a way of getting even when he or she is not cooperating. Of course, few people will admit that they are using the silent treatment as a controlling technique. They rationalize it as a normal reaction to failed communication or as a way of shutting down out of frustration.

It is true that there is a fine line between being silent because all else has been said and done (or because you are being contemplative), and using silence as a controlling technique in lieu of other more conducive forms of communication; however, it's important that we try to be sensitive to our motivations for being silent so we do not cross over that line.

SUGGESTIONS

- Become aware of when you are using the "silent treatment" to gain power in a relationship. When you catch yourself with hidden motivations for being quiet, break the ice and try to open lines of communication.

- Remember, it is all right to be silent in order to be contemplative, to take a break from arguing, or as an expression of exasperation; but don't use it as a way of getting even or of forcing someone to give in to you. Silence is not called for when someone is trying to communicate with you in order to work things out.

SEX

Sex has historically been a powerful way to keep your partner hooked or under control. There are names for this sort of control—seduction, bedroom politics or pillow talk. If love addicts have a sexual hold on their partner they will not hesitate to use it to keep a tight rein. Some love addicts rely so heavily on their ability to keep a partner "coming back for more," that they panic when there is something on the agenda besides making love. They feel unlovable if the relationship does not include sex, and worry about losing their partner if lovemaking grows stale.

SUGGESTIONS

- Don't use sex to get your way. Passion between people is wonderful, but it should be experienced and appreciated, not used as a way to control someone.

- Don't use sexuality to hold onto your partner. Consider other ways to promote a bond between you.

- Don't use a person's sexual attraction to you as a way to abate your fears of losing them to someone else. Face your fears.

- Don't get involved with people who are only physically attracted to you. It's too tempting to use sex as a way to control them.

- If your sexual desirability is linked to your self-esteem, work on believing that you have something to offer in a relationship besides sex.

NEGATIVE CARETAKING

Negative caretaking means doing for others what they should be doing for themselves; giving more than you are receiving; and taking on more than your share of the responsibility for the survival of a relationship. This can mean taking care of people's material needs, organizing their life, covering up for them, doing their work, finding them a job, making their decisions, bailing them out of trouble, ad infinitum.

For the most part, caretaking is an attempt to control the outcome of a relationship by trying to earn or "buy" love, affection, loyalty, attention, companionship, etc. If I take care of you will you love me? Caretaking may be the love addict's way of establishing a dependency situation so his or her partner is motivated to stay in the relationship. (He can't make it without me; she would be a fool to leave.) Love addicts behave this way because they feel unlovable or unworthy of attracting and sustaining love by being themselves or by offering their "fair share." They feel the need for some "trick up their sleeve," and for them this means sacrificing their needs to take care of their partner.

Negative caretaking is also the love addict's way of trying to control painful feelings. A love addict learns how easy it is to avoid feeling fear, anger, loneliness, or self-pity when they are distracted by the task of meeting other people's needs. (Most love addicts learned this in childhood. They grew up as rescuers in a dysfunctional home where caretaking was their way of trying to control the uncontrollable, anesthetize their pain, and validate their self-worth.)

SUGGESTIONS

- Acknowledge your role as a caretaker and look at your hidden motivations for being a caretaker. Write about it. Remember that suffering and sacrifice do not make someone appreciate you more. If your partner stays with you just because you are willing to take care of them, then you are not in a healthy relationship.

- Do some thinking and writing about appropriate give and take in a relationship. If you don't know what is appropriate, ask others or read some books.

- Believe that you deserve to be loved without having to earn it. Believe that you do not have to make someone dependent on you to be in a relationship. If your partner is the right person for you he or she will love you for a variety of reasons, including the fact that you provide companionship, sharing, etc.; but this is not the same as taking care of someone so he or she won't leave you.

- Learn where to draw the line regarding loyalty.

- Take action. Make some well-thought-out changes in your life. Take some risks.
  - Don't do for your partner what he should be doing for himself.
  - Let your partner take on her share of the responsibility for keeping the relationship going.
  - Insist on receiving as much as you give. (Learn when to be selfish—see Robin Norwood.)
  - Channel some of your need to be needed in other directions.

    If you have children, try to give them the nurturing they need. You may have deprived them in order to take care of your partner.

    Consider some sort of community service. "What the world needs now is love sweet love, not just for one but for everyone."

- If you are not already in a relationship:
  - Avoid potential partners who appear to be needy, even if you can identify with them. It is too tempting to become a caretaker to such people.
  - As you are getting to know someone look for the indications that he or she is needy or the kind of person who is looking for a caretaker.

    Don't give advice or be helpful right away, even if someone shares his or her problems. Wait and see if this person handles his or her own life maturely.

    Keep your praise or stroking at a minimum and see if this person knows how to stroke him or herself.

Don't rationalize or make excuses for people who can, but won't, take care of themselves.

Avoid saying things like "At least this person is not as bad as the last one," or "No one is perfect." For caretakers this can be the beginning of denial.

– Set your standards for give and take in a relationship prior to falling in love or getting involved with someone. When these standards are not met, walk away.

AN ATTACK OF HYSTERIA OR RAGE

An attack of hysteria or rage is an adult version of a temper tantrum. It is how love addicts attempt to recapture control when they feel that it is escaping their grasp. Typically, women get hysterical and men fly into a rage but these roles can be reversed. (Of course, hysteria is a passive-aggressive controlling technique like the others I have mentioned, but rage is an overt controlling device.)

Both hysteria and rage are characterized by excessive or uncontrollable emotion such as fear or panic, and can manifest themselves as irrational tears, laughter, anger, or violence. They can also be self-induced as a dramatic ploy, but they are usually a genuine reaction to desperation and fear. The paradox of hysteria and rage is that they are attempts to gain control by losing control.

As controlling techniques, both hysteria and rage are very effective because they can be very intimidating. People are easily convinced to give the hysterical or angry person whatever they need to calm them down.

SUGGESTIONS

• If you have a tendency to get hysterical or fly into a rage under stress, then consider the possibility that you might be unconsciously trying to take control of the situation in order to calm your fears. This is the "little child" within you who is overreacting to the stress, and you must learn to return to the "adult" ego state and nip your rising hysteria in the bud. You do have a choice.

• If you need something and your partner won't respond to your need, then let it go and talk about it later. Do not panic. Do not try to take control of the situation by becoming hysterical or violent. It only brings about a temporary reprieve or makes things worse. If your overall needs are not being met in the relationship, and long term negotiations are not effective, then you might just have to give up on this partnership.

• Consider the following techniques for staying calm when you feel an attack of hysteria or rage coming on:

  – Give yourself reassurance; or pray if you like.

  – Call a friend who understands or go for a walk.

  – Sit down and write about what you are feeling.

  – Learn to flow with the situation; let everything work itself out naturally.

  – If your partner is leaving then let him or her go. Tell yourself you are not being abandoned but that you both need time to sort things out.

The bottom line is this: nothing is worth having if you have to get hysterical or fly into a rage to get it.

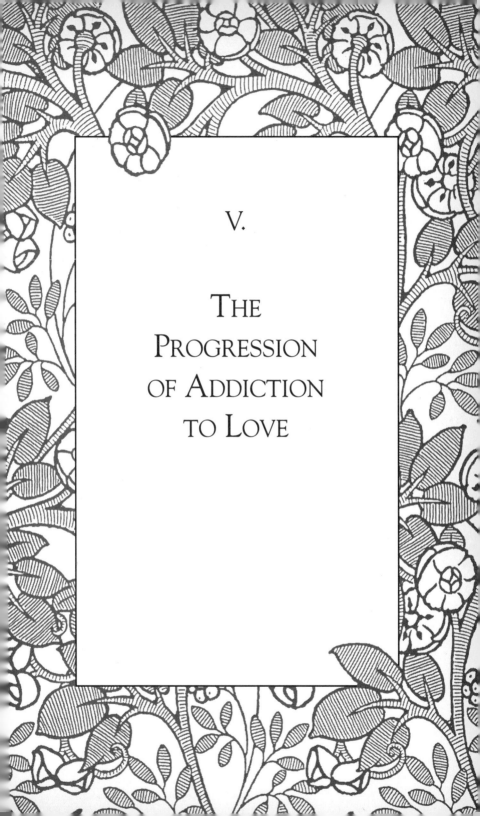

V.

The Progression of Addiction to Love

...the lover says, 'I cannot love anyone else, I cannot give up loving, I cannot give up this love, for it would be the death of me and I would die of love.'

SØREN KIERKEGAARD in *Works of Love*

CONTRIBUTING FACTORS

How fast and how far addiction to love can progress depends on:

- The love addict's level of attachment hunger—need
- The age of the love addict—diminishing self-esteem in a youth-oriented culture
- Failure heaped upon failure—mounting fears and diminished hope
- Level of denial—I don't have a problem
- Level of stubbornness about needing to change— I'll die trying
- Refusal to get help—pride
- Childhood experiences—trauma

BEGINNING STAGE

In the beginning stage the symptoms mentioned in Part IV are just tendencies. Love addicts still have their health, as well as a moderate amount of self-respect, and they will not hold on to a relationship too long if their needs are not being met.

CHRONIC STAGE

In the chronic stage the symptoms of addiction to love are a way of life. Love addicts experience one addictive relationship after another and stress-related emotional and physical problems have begun to develop. Also, subsidiary addictions will now start to become a problem because the love addict is trying to find ways to take the edge off of his or her emotional pain.

DYING FOR LOVE

As pointed out by Robin Norwood, in *Women Who Love Too Much*, obsessing in a relationship can not only cause physical and emotional problems, it can kill you. Death may come from stress related disorders (heart failure, strokes, ulcers, etc.), or from the violence that is often a part of an addictive relationship. Death may also come as a result of suicide.

TYPICAL PROGRESSION

- Childhood trauma occurs;
- An excessive hunger for love first appears;
- Low self-esteem begins to develop;
- A fear of abandonment and loneliness surfaces;
- Emotional pain becomes apparent;
- A need for relief increases;
- Mood altering experiences are used to relieve anxiety;
- Romantic fantasies become a fix;
- A preoccupation with romance becomes habitual;
- Relationships become a fix;

- Unhealthy dependencies begin to appear;
- An obsession with someone may occur;
- Addictive thoughts and behavior become ritualized;
- The patterns of addiction are repeated and become entrenched;
- Problems associated with obsession and dependency develop;
- Emotional distress appears;
- Health problems appear;
- Subsidiary addictions continue to progress;
- Addiction to love becomes a problem;
- The love addict loses control of his or her life;
- Chronic depression sets in;
- A crisis appears;
- A life-threatening situation develops;
- Danger is imminent;
- Death or intervention occurs.

Kathy

Kathy experienced a lot of trauma in her childhood including neglect, abandonment, incest, the death of her brother, and peer rejection.

As Kathy looks back over her childhood, she remembers feeling sad, lonely, rejected, angry, and ashamed. She doesn't ever remember being happy. To ease her emotional pain, she started fantasizing. It was a great escape. She dreamed about romantic love, meeting the perfect man someday, having a family, and living happily ever after. This fantasizing was a great diversion, but Kathy overdid it. She couldn't concentrate on what her teachers were saying because she was always looking out the window and daydreaming about finding her Prince Charming. She read romantic novels instead of textbooks and cut school to see romantic movies like "Splendor in the Grass." Her mother commented once that Kathy seemed to be overly preoccupied with romance.

Kathy was about ten years old when she started falling in love. Her first crush was on a boy named Alan. Kathy projected all of her romantic fantasies onto Alan—hoping that he would be the one to make her dreams come true. Then she started fantasizing about him all the time. Alan was embarrassed and angry that Kathy liked him so much. He told her not to write his name on her school books. He threw rocks at her when she walked by his house. Kathy also watched Alan play baseball at the park. Sometimes, she was the only spectator, but she never missed a game. At school, during recess, Kathy would sneak into the cloakroom and put on Alan's jacket. She wanted to touch something that was his—she wanted to smell his presence. She also wrote in her diary about her love for Alan. Day after day, she described the bittersweet pain of unrequited love, hoping that someday Alan would love her too.

Of course, there were other infatuations over the years. The pattern was always the same. Attraction led to fantasies of loving and being loved and a preoccupation with someone. This would be followed by the notion that only this particular boy could make Kathy happy. Then Kathy felt as if she had no choice in the matter. All of this led to an obsession and living in the future via her fantasies. Kathy always imagined that if she kept her love alive these boys would someday fall in love with her and her patience would be rewarded. This distorted thinking fueled her obsession and extended her heartache. Eventually, Kathy would get emotionally and physically sick from yearning to be with someone she could not have. Then, when the pain became unbearable, the obsession faded and she found someone more promising to adore from a distance.

The projection of her romantic fantasies onto one boy after another was the progression of Kathy's addiction to love. With this progression came problems. By this, I mean that her childhood fantasizing certainly eased her emotional pain, but the projection of these fantasies onto a particular person only brought pain. This is true of all addictions. The exhilarating, mood-altering experience that starts out as a painkiller becomes a liability. However, like other addicts, Kathy found herself unable to stop. She was hooked. Like the alcoholic who can't stop after one drink, Kathy couldn't stop after she fell in love. She had to obsess. She had to have her dreams come true. It took a lot for her to give up on her fantasies and obsessions.

High school was not a happy time for Kathy. She prayed that someone would ask her out for a date. One time she did get a call from a boy. He asked her out and she agreed to go. She was so excited and nervous that she stayed up all night making a new dress. The next day at school some boys snickered at her as she walked by, and that night someone called to tell her that the phone call she had gotten the night before was just a joke. Kathy was so embarrassed, she wanted to die. She prayed that no one would hear about what had happened.

When Kathy was nineteen years old, she became desperate to have a relationship. She wanted to have a boyfriend and she was willing to do anything to get one, even if she had to take someone hostage. Her addiction to love was progressing.

Because of her low self-esteem, Kathy did not feel loveable enough to attract someone she really liked, and she was too impatient to wait for someone compatible to come along, so she got involved with the first person who showed any interest in her.

Kathy met Ray at a bus stop. He was twenty five years old, unemployed, and living with his mother. Kathy started spending a lot of time with Ray and within a few months she was pregnant. She decided to sign up for government assistance (welfare) and find a place where she and Ray could live together. From that point on, Kathy became Ray's caretaker. She paid the bills, bought Ray's clothes and gave him money for drugs.

Kathy liked caretaking. It was her way of trying to control the outcome of the relationship by buying love and making Ray dependent on her so he would not leave. Kathy also liked caretaking because it made her feel benevolent, even superior. This gave her a false sense of self-esteem.

Caretaking also made Kathy feel needed or indispensable. It gave her an identity. She saw herself as Mother Teresa taking care of a lost soul who needed her guidance. Since Ray was a drug addict she tried to clean him up. Because he was a Viet Nam veteran, she tried to counsel him and care for his emotional wounds. Because he was abused as a child, she accepted it when he abused her. Whatever Ray's problem was, Kathy tried to fix it. Of course, she didn't realize that she should not be doing for Ray what he should be doing for himself; that she should not be trying to combine charity with intimacy. However, Kathy was doing the best she could at the time. She really didn't know any better—she was a love addict.

What Kathy liked most about caretaking was that it killed a lot of time and was a great distraction from her emotional pain (anger, shame, loneliness, depression, fear, low self-esteem, etc.) Her problems faded when she concentrated on Ray's problems. She did not see herself as negative or controlling. She did not see caretaking as a way to avoid recognizing that she had problems of her own—that Ray was not the only one who needed fixing. For her it was just a lifestyle, one shared by most of her friends.

As a caretaker and love addict, Kathy accepted a lot of neglect. She had a high tolerance for suffering because she was used to it, and because she thought this was the price she had to pay for having a man in her life. Ray took advantage of this. He only came home when he felt like it. He never helped to clean up. He didn't give Kathy any affection and their love-making was unstimulating. Kathy and Ray didn't even talk very much, unless Ray was telling her what to do. He also took all of her money, except what went to pay the bills. Sometimes Kathy would try to hide money for a rainy day. Then Ray would get into some kind of trouble with gambling or drugs and start yelling at Kathy to give him some money. If yelling didn't help, he would cry and tell Kathy he would be killed by the men he owed money to if she didn't help him. Kathy always gave in. She felt responsible for Ray.

Of course, Kathy wanted more than she was getting out of the relationship. She was just not ready to demand it or to find someone who was willing to offer her the love and support she needed. So she just cried when her birthday went unnoticed. When Ray didn't come home she just kept busy waiting for him to return. She baked, sewed, cleaned house, and took care of their daughter—anything to keep herself occupied so she didn't have to feel the pain she was in.

Kathy also accepted a lot of dishonesty from Ray. She had no idea what it felt like to trust him. Usually he lied to her about other women. He said he was not having affairs and he usually was. Deep down Kathy knew what was going on, but she buried her head in the sand because she was afraid if she said something to Ray he might leave her.

In her relationship with Ray, Kathy also lacked personality boundaries. She had no values or interests of her own. She adopted his mannerisms and speech patterns. She dressed the way he liked her to dress, and she did the things he wanted her to do. She listened to the music he liked, and she even talked herself into supporting the things he believed in—even if they were contrary to her own belief system.

Despite her dependency on this relationship, Kathy tried several times to end it. She remembers after six months of being with Ray that she wanted to leave him. When she told him she was going to leave he got very sad. He said, "I guess you've gotten what you want and now you're ready to move on and leave me behind." Kathy felt guilty when Ray said this and she stayed with him to keep from hurting his feelings. She projected her fear of being abandoned onto him, and assumed that he could not survive if she left him.

Later in the relationship, Kathy thought about leaving Ray again, but she felt guilty about withdrawing her financial support. Kathy knew Ray had become dependent on her.

Kathy was also afraid to leave the relationship because she knew it meant facing her fear of loneliness and giving up her identity as a caretaker. She knew it would mean going through a lot of emotional pain (withdrawal) so she just kept putting it off, hoping her misery would end someday.

Another time Kathy asked Ray to leave, but when he started packing his bags she panicked. The next thing she knew, she was begging Ray to stay—like a child begging her mother not to leave her alone in the dark. During this scene, Kathy's fear of abandonment overwhelmed her, and she was ready to do anything to avoid feeling the panic that gripped her heart.

While it seemed as if Kathy would never leave Ray, eventually she did fall in love with someone else and decided to ask Ray for a divorce. Unfortunately, Ray was not ready to lose Kathy. When she told him she was going to leave he held a knife up to her throat and threatened to kill her. Then he beat her up and held her prisoner in the house. He kept saying to her, "I know you still love me, just admit it." After three days, Kathy agreed to stay with Ray and he immediately calmed down. Then she said, "Ray it's time to cook dinner and I need to go to the store and get some things." Ray agreed to let Kathy go and she quickly hurried out of the door. Once she was safe, Kathy went to a phone booth and called the police. Ray was told by the police to leave the house and he did.

The man Kathy left Ray for was not much better, and that relationship failed too. From this point on, Kathy became involved in a series of short-term relationships similar to the one she had with Ray. All of these relationships failed because Kathy was too emotionally unstable to select an appropriate partner; and even if she did, she couldn't sustain a relationship because of her neediness, low self-esteem, and fear of abandonment. So, as the years passed, Kathy's hungry heart went unsatisfied and this made her even more desperate to find love.

As Kathy's addiction to love progressed, her health began to deteriorate. She developed a spastic colon and high blood pressure. She was chronically depressed and almost died in two car accidents. (The first time she couldn't see the road because she was crying and the second time she was fantasizing instead of looking where she was going.)

Once, after a failed relationship, Kathy was in so much pain she cut her wrists. This was not a suicide attempt. She didn't cut deep enough to do any damage. She just wanted her body to go into shock and ease her emotional pain for awhile. She was crying out for help.

When Kathy was thirty four years old she fell in love with a man that she worked with. She could not seem to get his attention, so she decided after years of being overweight that she would shed her excess pounds, become more attractive and seduce this man. It just started out as a simple diet. However, when Kathy started to look great and the man did not respond, she kept dieting. Eventually she became ill and had to be hospitalized. She later told her doctor: "I thought that if I lost five more pounds he would notice me; then it was five more pounds and he would love me." Then later I was so depressed it became: "five more pounds and he'll come to my grave and wish he had loved me." (This is controlling from the grave.)

As a result of this latest obsession, Kathy not only got ill from her anorexia, she sank into a deep depression and shut down emotionally. Her once-clean house became a pig sty. She yelled at her daughter and left her to take care of herself. She also started drinking every day to drown her sorrows and began to secretly plan her suicide. Kathy felt that life was not worth living without someone special, and yet somehow genuine love and healthy relationships had eluded her. Kathy was ready to die for love.

VI.

RECOVERY

A Brighter Tomorrow

Life may take a downward spiral;
And overwhelm us for awhile.
Pain may seem a way of life;
Endless moments filled with strife.
Gloom may settle in our souls;
Splitting that which once was whole.
And yet despite this painful rift;
There still exists a timeless gift.
The saving grace when all is gray;
The promise of a brand new day.

Courageously Facing Your Own Shortcomings

Through the mist, into the sun; step by step—I cannot run.

Anyone recovering from his or her battle with an obsession knows how it feels to be tired of being sick and tired. This is the painful last stage of holding on to old ideas. Hopefully, what comes of this is the courage to admit defeat and a willingness to change one's way of thinking and behaving. For love addicts, this is the moment at which they are ready to move on. As Robin Norwood puts it, "All the struggles, drama and chaos of the past have lost their appeal." The love addict has finally had enough.

Once love addicts are ready to face their problems (their addiction), they come to the second most difficult hurdle on their road to recovery—admitting their part in the creation of these problems. Whether we like to acknowledge it or not, when things go wrong in our lives it is because we have said or done something at some point to get the ball rolling. Note the following message from Irene de Castillejo, in her book *Knowing Woman*, about how our outer world responds to our inner frame of mind.

Everyone knows those horrible days when everything goes wrong. One just misses the train, one's boss is in a bad temper, the bus conductor is rude and the shop assistants refuse to serve one. If one is capable of being objective at all on such a day, admittedly rather a difficult feat, one knows that at the root of the trouble lies one's own negative mood. Like calls to like. In intimate relationships it is fundamental to know that it is one's own inner attitude of mind which...actually influences the reaction of one's partner. For instance, the wife who complains of a bullying husband has generally brought it upon herself by a cringing attitude. In fact her own unconscious tendency to cringe will have caused her to choose a bully for a mate. If she can learn to stand up for herself it is extremely likely that, after the first shock of dismay at being thwarted, the husband's disdain will turn to admiration, even though he may keep his admiration to himself.... Similarly, the wife who despairs of her husband's inability to understand her, needs to recognize that she has not only failed to tell him what she means, she has probably failed to tell herself. Women's own confusion today about who they are and what they want of life causes a fog around them which confuses everyone. Far more important than an uttered declaration of her meaning is her own inner clarity.

If we can go as far as admitting our own partial responsibility for outer conditions we have already entered that path towards freedom where we need be no longer the blind, impotent victim of our environment.

If the way love addicts think and behave affect the way people respond to them, they must begin to challenge their old ways of thinking and behaving. To do this they must evaluate themselves and pinpoint the exact feelings, values, thoughts, and actions which cause them to be drawn into addictive loving. With this in mind, it is recommended that love addicts in recovery make a personal inventory of their "shortcomings" or an analysis of their addiction. There is more than one way to do this, but it is recommended that it be a written inventory. Love addicts might use the list of symptoms in this book as their guide, responding to each one as it speaks to their particular condition. Or they can find a support group and make notes of what they learn about themselves. They might even take daily notes as they observe themselves and then expound on it later.

Whatever methods love addicts use to prepare their inventory, they should remember to be as thorough and honest as possible. They should mention the feelings, values, thoughts, and types of behavior that are causing the problems (with examples) and then explore their motivations and new-found awareness of this as a liability rather than an asset. They might even want to write about specific changes they want to make (goals). Most of all they need to remember that it is not *how* you do an inventory that counts, but the fact that you *do* it at all. Taking action is the key to recovery.

MAKING CHANGES

I shall be telling this with a sigh
Somewhere ages and ages hence:
Two roads diverged in a wood, and I—
I took the one less traveled by,
And that has made all the difference

ROBERT FROST

Making changes is the next step in recovery. Changes include outer modifications of behavior and an inner shift in values and thinking patterns. The changes love addicts make will be based on the insights they have gained while preparing their inventory, and they should remember that the person they need to change is themselves.

If changing is crucial, where does the willingness to change come from? No one really knows. Some love addicts never find the willingness to change. They live in a state of denial all of their lives. Other love addicts are only in the early stages of addiction to love, and yet they want to change. All they need is some help.

Most love addicts end up suffering quite a bit before they are willing to change. It takes a lot for them to get their act together.

There are also those people who have some willingness to change, but not enough. They may work at a program of recovery for awhile, but they don't stick with it. I met one such love addict a few years ago. I was teaching my class and she walked in late. She had a black eye and broken arm. I talked with her after the class and she was grateful to have found her way to me. It turned out that she was addicted to an abusive man. I worked with this woman for a few weeks, but, unfortunately, she couldn't pull herself out of her downward spiral. A few weeks later she killed herself.

No one really knows why some love addicts are willing to change, and others are not; but if that magic moment finally arrives, recovery has begun.

When love addicts are ready to change, they should do the easy things first to build up their confidence and then other changes will follow. Success builds upon success. Sometimes inner changes come from outer changes, and sometimes outer changes are a by-product of inner changes.

SUGGESTIONS

- Recognize when you do something you do not want to do. Awareness is the beginning of change.

- Identify and make a list of alternative behaviors.

- Substitute a good habit for a bad one.

- Don't make excuses or procrastinate. Start now.
- Give yourself encouragement—affirmations.
- Seek advice and help from others.
- Join a support group.
- Make a commitment to a friend or support group (verbalization can really help).
- *Avoid* companions who do not support you.
- Find new role models.
- Remember: *action* leads to *motivation* leads to *more action*
- Remember: change is a process; it takes time. Be patient.
- Avoid negative attitudes that inhibit change. The glass is half full not half empty.
- Break down the changes you want to make into manageable steps (make a list).
- Visualize the results; become goal oriented.
- If you are a spiritual or religious person and believe in grace, divine intervention and/or the power of prayer, then by all means pray for a little push to take action.

PROGRESS NOT PERFECTION

We claim spiritual progress rather than spiritual perfection.

ALCOHOLICS ANONYMOUS

When your body is hurt it takes a certain amount of time to heal. Everyday, if you take care of yourself, you get a little healthier. Recovery from addiction to love also takes a certain amount of time. Depending on the seriousness of the addiction, recovery can take years. This is a bitter disappointment to many recovering love addicts, because many of them want to get well overnight or at the very moment they recognize their problem. I call this attitude magical thinking—the idea that our fairy god mother is going to whisk her magic wand and suddenly transform us.

Unfortunately, recovery does not happen overnight. It is a slow, tedious process fraught with many pitfalls. It also includes some pain. However, unlike the pain suffered by the *practicing* love addict, the pain of recovery leads somewhere. It is the pain of growth and it leads to happiness and freedom.

Making changes is a process that goes through various stages. For love addicts, the first stage is knowledge or awareness—recognizing their addictive patterns. The next stage is implementing new ways of handling situations. This will happen slowly and require a lot of practice. First recovering love addicts will notice distorted behavior, thoughts, and values in *hindsight*. Then they will try to correct their mistakes. Later they will start recognizing addictive patterns *as they are occurring*, but they will still be unable to restrain themselves. Eventually, love addicts are able to put a halt to their addictive patterns in mid-stride and finally there will come a time when they see the distorted thoughts and behavior coming on, and find new ways of handling the situation. When this happens a new skill has been learned, a skill which can now be practiced and integrated into the recovering love addict's life.

This is the beginning of recovery. The temptation to act out addictively is identified and suppressed. Then a new skill is implemented and the recovering love addict becomes stronger. This newfound strength brings on a surge of confidence, which in turn energizes love addicts and makes it easier for them to practice even more self-restraint. In later stages of recovery, *non-addictive* behavior becomes habitual, and this successful behavior modification contributes to an inner transformation taking place within the recovering love addict. Suddenly, there is a wealth of newly acquired self-respect which pushes aside that sense of powerlessness. Fears subside, and a sense of happiness and freedom become readily apparent. It is as if the recovering love addict has been reborn.

Changing not only takes time, recovering love addicts will also go through this process with one issue after another. Just as they get one addictive behavior under control there will be something new to deal with. Therefore, love addicts must be patient with themselves, and look for signs of progress, not perfection. Perhaps they have reworked their addictive *values* with regard to romantic love and relationships, but they may still have trouble changing their addictive *behavior*. This is progress. Maybe the last time they were addicted to someone they were abused. Now they get hooked on nice people who just can't make a commitment. This is progress. Maybe it used to be impossible to end an addictive relationship and now it is just difficult. This is progress, and progress is how recovering love addicts must measure their recovery. Every now and then they must ask themselves if they have made progress. If the answer is yes, then they are doing fine.

It is important to understand that recovery is not perfect because people are not perfect; and no one handles all their personal affairs perfectly. Some people, more than others, lack the tools they need to be satisfied in their relationships. Therefore, they must honestly evaluate what they are missing and work to develop new skills which will help them have richer more fulfilling relationships. They will not, however, do this perfectly or overnight.

It is not my intention to discourage recovering love addicts by pointing out that getting healthier takes a long time. I just believe it is better to understand how long the process takes, and courageously accept this, than to give up trying because there is no miraculous recovery. Addiction to love is a powerful and insidious disorder. It springs from childhood trauma that at best can only be transcended, not reversed. And healing takes time. Therefore, I encourage love addicts to be patient with themselves.

THERAPY AND SUPPORT GROUPS
REALLY DO HELP

If we are painstaking about this phase of our development, we will be amazed before we are halfway through. We are going to know a new freedom and a new happiness. We will not regret the past nor wish to shut the door on it. We will comprehend the word serenity and we will know peace.

ALCOHOLICS ANONYMOUS

Recovery requires a certain environment. It cannot be obtained by reading a book and expecting a magical transformation. It can only be obtained by working hard with the helpful guidance of those who understand the problem of obsession and dependency in relationships. Therefore, love addicts in recovery should go for help.

Help can be found in therapy and/or support groups. Both these environments are conducive to recovery for the following reasons:

- In therapy and support groups love addicts can be honest and share secrets. This has always been therapeutic for people who are bearing the burden of so much inner turmoil.

- Therapy and support groups provide a place to learn how addiction to love manifests itself. Love addicts learn *how* their addiction gets started, *when* it gets started, and *what* the symptoms are. Most of all, love addicts learn what can be done about the problem—how to initiate and *maintain* recovery.

- Therapy and support groups provide love addicts with a lot of badly needed unconditional love. In early recovery, love addicts do not know how to love themselves. However, a therapist or support group can do for them what they cannot yet do for themselves. They can provide the unconditional love that promotes recovery— the acceptance that will someday be transformed into self-love. M. Scott Peck, in *The Road Less Traveled*, puts it this way. "It is obvious, then, that in order to be healed through psychotherapy, the patient must receive at least a portion of the genuine love of which the patient was deprived [in childhood]. If the psychotherapist cannot genuinely love a patient, genuine healing will not occur." Put another way, "If I speak in the tongues of men and of angels, but have not love, I am a noisy gong." Corinthians 13:1

- Therapy and support groups provide a working environment which guard against procrastination and denial. Even on those bleak days when recovering love addicts are resisting the truth, they know deep down they would not be in therapy or a support group if they didn't have a problem.

- Support groups and therapy help love addicts recognize a slip or relapse.

- Calling people in their support group can help recovering love addicts avoid dysfunctional behavior. Like the alcoholic who calls his sponsor in Alcoholics Anonymous before he takes that first drink, the love addict can be advised by someone in his or her support group not to get married on the third date.

Not only do recovering love addicts need help, they need it on a regular basis. One of the most common mistakes recovering love addicts make is to prematurely drop out of therapy or support groups. Sometimes they do this because of complacency. They don't think they have a problem anymore, or they feel strong enough to make it on their own. This attitude can easily lead to regression. Sometimes love addicts are discouraged by the slow pace of recovery. They just get tired of struggling, so they drop out.

Whatever prompts love addicts to drift away from an environment conducive to recovery, they should be warned that addiction to love is an insidious problem, learned early and practiced well. It does not just disappear one day. For a long time, maybe forever, it goes into remission, and it takes constant vigilance to keep it in that inactive state.

It may be disconcerting to find out that there is probably no permanent cure for addiction to love. Still, in my experience this is usually the case. The struggle may get easier, but there is always the possibility of regression. This does not mean that love addicts will always be in therapy, or always have to attend a support group. It just means that recovering love addicts must not be in a hurry to discard their support system. It could take years for them to reach a point where the changes brought about in recovery can survive without the support of those who have helped them along the way; and by always placing themselves in the company of people working toward continued recovery, love addicts are giving themselves the best opportunity to succeed. Good soil and tender loving care produce lovely flowers, and therapy or support groups provide the optimum environment for recovery from addiction to love.

One note of caution. While therapy and support groups are important, love addicts need to be selective. Not all therapists and support groups will be helpful with the problems of love addicts. The correct approach is to shop around and watch for progress as a way of measuring the effectiveness of the therapeutic environment that you have chosen.

Recovery

HEALING THE WOUNDS OF CHILDHOOD TRAUMA

Grief Work

All healing is release from the past...It is enough to heal the past and make the future free. It is enough to let the present be accepted as it is.

A Course In Miracles

Most love addicts have survived some form of childhood trauma. In recovery, they must make an effort to heal the wounds of the past. They must also accept the fact that this is an inside job. Nothing outside of themselves is going to heal them. Therapy and support groups are supportive environments, but love addicts have to do all the work to promote their own inner healing.

Healing the wounds of the past is a long and drawn out process. This process begins when recovering love addicts accept the fact that they were traumatized. Many people are in *denial* about this. They don't remember what really happened. They have blocked out the truth because it is too painful, or they see what happened to them as normal because they have nothing to compare it with.

Trauma is any experience which interferes with the feeling of safety and security that children need as they are growing up—any disruption to the child's well-being that is not worked through within the family unit via honesty, love, and communication. The following experiences are considered traumatic:

- Neglect and abandonment—no matter how young you were when it happened.

- Abuse—this is hitting, beating, or sexual violation, and it can occur at *home*, *school*, or in *church*.

- Toxic shame—this is being told that you are intrinsical-
ly bad.

- Emotional (covert) incest—this is an unhealthy
enmeshment with a parent.

- Keeping secrets from children about family problems.

- Forcing children to keep secrets—this happens a lot in
alcoholic homes.

- Refusing to let children express their feelings.

- Peer rejection or not having any friends.

- Unintentional trauma—this can be:

  – a very frightening experience like getting lost;

  – a death in the family;

  – a serious accident;

  – a prolonged illness;

  – accidently hurting someone else seriously.

  – Anything that severely disturbs your sense of security.

- Unhealthy mirroring or role modeling—parents are like
mirrors, and children define themselves by what they
see in that mirror. Parents who are shame-based or have
low self-esteem reflect a negative image to their children who then conclude that they are flawed as well.
This is how parents pass on shame and low self-esteem
even though they are trying to be good parents.

Children are usually not capable of discerning trauma because
they have an unconscious need to see everything as being all
right. They suffer and feel pain, but at the same time they find
a mechanism whereby they deny or suppress the reality of
their environment. This distortion of the truth (denial) is
how they survive emotionally. However, as adults, these traumatized children have to break through the magical illusion

that everything in their childhood was all right. Even if they don't remember what happened, if they have the symptoms of childhood trauma, it is safe to assume they have been traumatized. Some of the symptoms of childhood trauma are:

- low self-esteem
- unstable relationships
- lack of impulse control
- self-destructive behavior
- mood swings
- uncontrollable outbursts of anger
- self-mutilation
- suicide attempts
- feelings of alienation
- chronic feelings of emptiness
- lack of a strong sense of identity
- fear of abandonment
- anxiety/panic attacks
- chronic depression
- delusional thinking
- shame
- self-absorption
- chronic loneliness
- chronic hopelessness or apathy
- feelings of helplessness
- chronic insomnia
- hypochondria
- retarded emotional growth

Once recovering love addicts stop denying that they experienced some form of childhood trauma, it can be helpful if they *identify* the nature of that trauma. Was it sustained or intermittent? Was it neglect or abuse? Was it at home or at school? What was going on, and who were the people involved? Some love addicts will know the answers to these questions and others will not. It can also be helpful to read some books about childhood trauma or personality disorders. It is amazing how many forms of trauma can occur, both inside and outside the home.

If love addicts can't remember much about their childhood, it might help if they talk to people who were there at the time (friends or family). Sometimes these people will not want to cooperate, but it's worth a try. Therapy can also help recovering love addicts identify what happened to them during their childhood. A therapist can draw out the truth in a safe environment and help interpret the facts. If the truth never gets revealed or validated, recovering love addicts should still go on with the healing process. They can refer to their trauma as "something that happened," even if they don't remember what that "something" was.

Once recovering love addicts have begun to identify their past trauma, they must learn to *talk* about it to someone they trust. This can be a therapist, a friend, or another recovering love addict in their support group—anyone who can be trusted to listen without judgement. Talking is part of the healing process because sharing our deepest, darkest secrets brings them out of the unconscious and into the conscious. Once this happens, the trauma can be worked through. Of course, talking also makes people feel better, but most of all it promotes self-awareness and understanding—both important steps in the healing process.

At this point, *writing* can help recovering love addicts. Key memories can flow when pen is put to paper, and the documentation of these truths can be useful later on. Writing is also a good way to get in touch with deep-seated feelings about what happened. Writing can mean keeping an ongoing journal about the recovery process, or taking an inventory of what happened with regard to the trauma and how it affected the love addict's life.

The hard part of the healing process comes when it is time for recovering love addicts to *feel* the pain of the past. Up to this point, they have been trying to dig up the memories of the past. When they are successful there is apt to be a strong emotional response. These feelings will vary from person to person, but some of the most common emotions felt at this time are anger, shock, anxiety, sadness, and depression. No matter how painful these feelings might be, it is important not to run away from them. These emotions have to be felt in full force, as if one were reliving the trauma once again. When these feelings come up, it is important to remember that they will pass and that this experience is just one stage in the healing process. I cannot say how long it will take for the feelings to pass, but if they are embraced rather than repressed they will subside.

To move on, to get away from these feelings, recovering love addicts must learn *acceptance*. Acceptance is the willingness to make peace with the fact that the trauma happened and that nothing the love addict does in the present can change the past. Acceptance is the willingness to live with the cards one has been dealt. The pain begins to subside with acceptance, so it is an important step. It is a hard step, but this is what it takes to begin feeling better.

Forgiveness is the next stage in the healing process. No matter how bad things were in the past, recovering love addicts cannot let go of the trauma unless they forgive those who hurt them. This does not mean they have to like the people that hurt them. It does not mean they have to associate with them. It just means they must "renounce [their] resentment or anger" (*American Heritage Dictionary*).

Forgiveness, like acceptance, is hard for many people. They struggle with their feelings of anger and it seems impossible to forgive. I suggest to these people that they keep trying to move to this level of the healing process, because peace of mind comes with forgiveness. Therefore, they should leave no stone unturned when trying to move to this level of the healing process. If they are religious this might help. Christians, for instance, believe that forgiving someone leads to the forgiveness of their own transgressions.

If it will help you to let go of your anger, have some sort of confrontation with the people in your childhood who hurt you. Write a letter; have a face-to-face conversation; or act out a confrontation in therapy. (Don't have any expectations about a face-to-face confrontation. It may help or it may not. Sometimes it can even make things worse if the people you confront attack you.)

If a confrontation doesn't work, love addicts should be patient, but think about the reward of forgiveness—freedom. Then there will come a time when the burden of resentment becomes too much to bear and forgiveness will just happen. From this point on, there will be periodic relapses, when the anger and sadness reappear, but these emotions will not be a daily frame of mind.

The final stage of the healing process is *letting go*. This is when recovering love addicts not only put down the burden of unwanted emotions associated with past trauma, but they let go of this burden and walk away. They have faced the truth, identified the trauma, talked about the pain, written about it, accepted what cannot be changed, and forgiven those who persecuted them. Now, they must take the freedom they have worked so hard to attain and move on to the next phase of their life. In other words, they must learn to live in the present unaffected by the past.

Healing will be easier if recovering love addicts try to see the good events of their past as well as the bad. Usually their childhood was a mixture of pain and happiness. That is, as much as recovering love addicts suffered, they were also blessed in some small ways. If there is absolutely nothing to be grateful for, recovering love addicts should at least see the good that has come out of their struggle to put the past in its place. Good does come out of bad, and from their struggle with diversity, love addicts have learned wisdom and coping skills—things that can help them for the rest of their lives.

Healing the wounds of the past takes time and patience. There is no set schedule. Healing is also a *process*, and recovering love addicts cannot skip over any of the stages. They cannot jump from identifying the trauma to forgiving those who hurt them. They have to go through the feeling stage before they can work on acceptance, forgiveness, and letting go. It is especially important for love addicts to feel their anger. Still, no matter how long the journey takes, or how many obstacles love addicts have to overcome, someday the wounds of the past will be healed. The memories will remain, but the pain will subside and no longer disrupt the love addict's daily life. And most of all, the pain of the past will no longer lead to anesthetizing experiences that become addictions.

SUMMARY
(Consider memorizing this process to make it more accessible in a crisis.)

- Identify trauma
- Talk
- Write
- Feel

- Accept
- Forgive
- Look at the bright side
- Move on

THE ETERNAL CHILD WITHIN

Except that you turn and become like a little
child you cannot enter the kingdom of heaven

MATTHEW 18:3

Children who are loved (given attention, strokes, guidance, comfort, and benevolent discipline) become filled with a feeling of well-being that sustains them in adulthood. This feeling of well-being manifests itself as self-esteem, confidence, maturity, and creativity. Children who are not loved do not have this feeling of wholeness and well-being, and their emotional development gets interrupted and fixated. As a result, they remain traumatized children or what I call *adult children*.

Healing the wounds of childhood trauma, as described in the previous chapter, helps recovering love addicts face their past and work through the painful feelings associated with it. This process is a freeing experience, but it does not always complete the healing process. Even when the anger is gone, and recovering love addicts are ready to move on with their lives, they still have to face the challenge of growing up.

One way for love addicts to deal with their immaturity is to *reparent* their inner child. The inner child is that part of the personality that retains the memories and feelings of childhood. The inner child is distinct from the adult personality, and in love addicts this inner child is wounded. He or she embodies all the trauma the love addict suffered as a child.

There are several great books about reparenting the inner child; therefore, I will not try to provide in one chapter what others describe in entire books. However, let me at least give you an idea of what reparenting the inner child is all about.

Kathy

When we left Kathy she was ready to die for love. Fortunately, she was able to avoid that fate by getting some help. At the recommendation of her friends and family, Kathy began seeing a therapist who helped her understand the relationship between her childhood and her addiction to love. Eventually, she even joined a 12-step support group and met other people who were recovering love addicts.

Over the next few months Kathy made a concerted effort to change her addictive behavior and heal the wounds of her childhood. As part of the healing process, Kathy also nurtured the traumatized little girl within her. She began this process by searching her memory for an image of her inner child, aided by an old photograph. At first, Kathy could not see her inner child. Then one day, while in a relaxed meditative state, she finally began to see herself as an adult sitting on a park bench looking at her inner child playing off in the distance. Her inner child (*little Kathy*) had a scowl on her face and was kicking the dirt with her feet. Obviously she was angry.

In her imagination, Kathy was able to interact with her inner child. First, she called to her, but *little Kathy* would not come. After awhile, *little Kathy* looked at Kathy out of the corner of her eye. Finally, she began to move in Kathy's direction. Then, still angry, *little Kathy* finally stood before her new mother who reached out and stroked her hair. This gesture broke through *little Kathy's* anger and she began to cry. Then Kathy held *little Kathy* in her arms and rocked her back and forth. After a while, *little Kathy* sauntered off to play, but she came back now and then to touch Kathy's hand and to see if she was still there. Kathy vowed at that moment to never leave her little girl again. She would be *little Kathy's* loving parent, and give her all the love she needed.

After this, Kathy initiated a dialogue between herself and her inner child. In other words, she began talking to herself. She began telling *little Kathy* in a hundred ways that she was lovable and should not be ashamed of herself. She also started validating *little Kathy's* feelings. She told her that it was all right to have negative emotions. She told her that negative emotions are a part of who we are and that to be healthy we must acknowledge the whole spectrum of feelings from happiness to depression.

As Kathy got to know her inner child more intimately, she discovered a lot about *little Kathy's* strengths and weaknesses. *Little Kathy* was intelligent, but undisciplined. Self-restraint was almost impossible for her, and when she got her feelings hurt she lashed out at people or withdrew and isolated. Suddenly, Kathy realized that *little Kathy* needed more than nurturing; she needed someone to set limits with her.

To begin setting limits with *little Kathy* (restraining her whims), Kathy developed a strong adult personality which could override the immature, childish part of herself. Then, she let this adult part of her personality take charge. For example, if *little Kathy* got afraid or angry, and wanted to act out in some negative way, Kathy said, "I understand that you are afraid and angry. However, let's work this through in a sensible way. Let's not act out compulsively right now." Then Kathy let the adult part of herself make the decision as to what to do next.

This way of dealing with her inner child was very effective for Kathy. In the beginning she had to use this technique many times a day. However, today Kathy senses an integration of her adult personality with that of her inner child. She doesn't always have to override her little girl's anxieties or veto negative behavior. For the most part, these childish fears and the desire to act out aren't there anymore. Kathy sees this as progress or maturation, but she does not think her inner child has gone away. She thinks that *little Kathy* will always be with her in some form.

BUILDING SELF-ESTEEM

When the melancholic dejectedly desires to be rid of life, of himself, is this not because he will not learn earnestly and rigorously to love himself? When a man surrenders himself to despair because the world or some person has left him faithlessly betrayed, what then is his fault except that he does not love himself the right way.

SØREN KIERKEGAARD in *Works of Love*

Love addicts lack self-esteem. This is at the heart of their problems with relationships and has to be corrected.

SUGGESTIONS

- I want to start out by saying that recovering love addicts have to work harder than most people to reclaim their self-esteem, and twice as hard to keep it. It would be nice if once we felt good about ourselves we could maintain that feeling, but usually it doesn't work out that way. Self-esteem can be elusive. One minute it's there, and the next minute it seems to have vanished. I would also like to point out that while many of the following suggestions will help you build up your self-esteem by *validating yourself*, other recommendations will encourage you to utilize the validation of others to enhance your self-esteem. This may seem contradictory. Many people feel that we can love ourselves unconditionally from within and have no need for the love of others. However, I feel that we do need some outer validation. We are only human, and no matter how strongly we believe in ourselves we need a little support. What is important to remember, is that our own *validation of ourselves* should come *first* and it is *more important* than what others think of us. In other words, you should build a strong foundation before you build a house.

- Adopt an attitude of self-acceptance or unconditional self-love. This means really understanding that you are a worthy person despite your shortcomings. This is a mind-set.

- Once you have a general acceptance of your worth as a human being, spend some time focusing on your specific attributes. This enhances your self-worth.

- As part of your new positive-thinking campaign, learn how to superimpose new information over your old negative tapes. (Negative tapes are all the hurtful and inappropriate things people said about you while you were growing up.) This is the best way to diminish inappropriate self-criticism which erodes self-esteem.

- Reclaim your self-respect—the pride or satisfaction that comes from:
  - Self-discipline
  - Being responsible
  - Honoring your own value system (By this I mean that if you value honesty you must be honest in order to feel good about yourself.)
  - Handling adversity well (Carl Jung said: "Neurosis is always a substitute for legitimate suffering.")

- Self-respect, which is a kind of conditional love, does not necessarily contradict the notion that you should love yourself unconditionally. Both concepts are important to maintain self-esteem. You must try to find the balance between loving yourself unconditionally and pushing yourself to do things that will engender self-respect.

- Surround yourself, whenever possible, with people who affirm you (people who like you just the way you are). Like it or not, your relationship with others can erode your self-esteem. So make a point of choosing your friends carefully. You did not have a choice about this as a child, but as an adult you are free to pick and choose your companions.

- Consider reading books about building up your self-esteem. This promotes self-awareness which is an important step in overcoming low self-esteem. (My favorite book is *Celebrating Yourself* by Dorothy Corkill Briggs.)

- Get to know yourself—who you are, your values, needs,

wants, taste, etc. How can you value what you do not know?

- Stop trying to be perfect. No one is perfect. We all live in the shadow of perfection, and are perfectly imperfect.

- Do nice things for yourself. Take care of yourself.

- At the same time, do nice things for other people now and then. There should be some balance in your life between taking care of yourself *and* being kind to others.

- Stop comparing yourself to others. They broke the mold when they made you, and this is the attitude you must have about yourself.

- Learn how to receive, especially if you are a people pleaser or have always had a monopoly on giving. Stop dismissing compliments and returning gifts. Let the love come in.

- Be creative. Everyone has a talent, and they should use it. This stimulates self-satisfaction and reinforces the positive things you have been thinking about yourself. John Bradshaw makes this point in his book, *Creating Love*. He says that "we grow in self-love as we see our work accepted by others." Just be cautious: if you share your work with others, choose people you trust—people who have the ability to see the beauty of what you are doing and if you get negative comments don't stop being creative. Appreciate your talents yourself. They are an expression of your innermost being and therefore beautiful.

- Stand up for yourself, especially if you don't usually do this. Remember that you value what you take care of. Standing up for yourself means:
  - Setting limits (saying no)

- Expressing your opinion
- Walking away from neglect or abuse
- Being assertive when appropriate
- No longer apologizing when you haven't done any-
  thing wrong

• Make amends if you have "wreckage from the past."
  Most love addicts have hurt people at one time or
  another, and they should honor their *appropriate* guilt.
  We have a conscience for a reason. You cannot ignore
  healthy guilt if you want to feel good about yourself.
  So, take the time to separate inappropriate guilt from
  healthy guilt and proceed accordingly.

• To protect your newfound self-esteem, prepare yourself
  mentally for those times when people try to drag you
  down (people you can't avoid like family and co-workers). Learn how to keep from taking them so seriously,
  as well as how to filter out inappropriate criticism.

SPIRITUALITY AND RECOVERY

*If, on the other hand, love undergoes the
transformation of the eternal...it does not
become characterized by habit; habit can
never get power over it. To what is said of
eternal life, that there is no sighing and no
tears, one can add: there is no habit.*

SØREN KIERKEGAARD,
in *Works of Love*

Your soul is oftentimes a battlefield upon
which your reason and your judgement wage
war against your passion....

KAHLIL GIBRAN in *The Prophet*

Recovery is difficult. It means doing things that are unfamiliar and frightening. It means facing the unknown. To help with this dilemma, I suggest that recovering love addicts consider getting in touch with their spiritual nature—that "vital principle or animating force traditionally believed to be within living beings." I recommend this because somehow tapping into this rich inner resource transforms us, or alters our attitudes and feelings to the extent that we can change what we have never been able to change before. This transformation is a vital part of the love addict's recovery.

Spirituality, or a relationship with a "Higher Power," can also give recovering love addicts the unconditional love and acceptance they were denied as children.

How spirituality works is a mystery. It is something that is often observed but not necessarily understood. I have seen people overcome their addictions with the aid of spirituality. They start out at the mercy of their dependencies. They are powerless over their inner compulsions and have no strength to fight back. They habitually re-enact behavior that is self-destructive and life-threatening. Then, in a moment of agony, they call out "God help me," and somewhere deep in their soul they surrender. They admit they are powerless and they ask for help. Then, sometimes quickly and sometimes slowly, they are filled with the power of the spirit and...

- They feel willing, when before they felt hesitant.

- They feel courageous, when before they felt terrified.

- They feel guided, when before they felt lost.

- They feel loved, when before they felt abandoned.

- They feel wise, when before they felt confused;
- They feel hopeful, when before they felt despair.
- They feel as if they are at the start of a glorious new journey, when before they felt near death.

Spirituality can also dissipate the obsession love addicts have with romantic love and intimacy. Once again, this is a phenomenon that is observed more than it is understood. I have observed God-conscious people just naturally become less interested in romantic love and more interested in other forms of life-sustaining love. Along with their new love of a Higher Power, spiritual people become interested in helping others in a non-codependent way (brotherly love); they discover the warmth of friendship (platonic love); they allow their love for parents, children, and siblings to blossom (familial love); and they begin to love themselves, often for the first time. It is as if their values have changed and they see the world with new eyes. Romantic love is not everything to them anymore. It is not an obsession. It is just *one* of life's many ways to experience love. This is a crucial step in recovery.

There is more than one way to have a spiritual awakening. For some people it will happen suddenly during one dramatic moment, a moment from which there is no turning back. For others it happens slowly. Over time, they just find themselves with a new attitude about a Higher Power and spirituality. Their closed mind becomes open and curious. They pray and they feel connected to their Higher Power. Or they act "as if" a Higher Power exists, and in time they come to believe. Some people practice meditation to find a Higher Power. Others may read spiritual literature or talk to people about spirituality. Whatever they do, recovering love addicts must do it repetitively, and they must not give up. If they are really seeking spirituality with an open mind, they will find it. If they really ask for spirituality with a humble heart, it will be given to them.

Finding spirituality is one step. Holding onto it is another. Spirituality tends to recede if left unattended. Traditionally, spirituality can be retained, and even enhanced, by keeping the channel of communication open between the provider of spirituality (God or Higher Power) and the receiver of spirituality (yourself). This means using such spiritual tools as prayer, meditation, repentance, compassion, charity, forgiveness, spiritual literature, and surrendering to God's will—whatever seems suitable or comfortable.

Some people will want to reinforce their budding spirituality with a supportive group—church or 12-step program. (For more information about the 12 steps and 12-step programs see Appendices.) This is optional, but spiritual fellowship can be very fulfilling. However, be warned that even within a group spirituality is a personal experience. Spirituality means searching the deep recesses of your mind, and finding a spiritual power that can lead you to a new level of consciousness. Standing in the light of another person's faith is not enough to promote recovery.

While spirituality is not mandatory, I recommend the spiritual path to love addicts because it makes recovery easier.

SUGGESTIONS FOR BEGINNERS

Spirituality means activating, or getting in touch with, that part of our psyche that connects us to a power greater than ourselves (greater than our fear). It means getting in touch with the "eternal" via our own "inner light." To do this, to embrace spirituality and receive the gift of psychological healing that goes with it, here are some suggestions:

- Acknowledge a power greater than yourself.

- Be open to the experience of spirituality. Allow the process to begin by discarding your prejudices. To paraphrase Herbert Spencer, ignorance is contempt prior to investigation.

- Do not confuse spirituality with religion, theology, or church; it is a personal experience between you and God.

- Read about spirituality (anything and everything).

- Seek out spiritual people and spiritual organizations.

- Once the door has sprung open (or even before), begin talking to God (prayer) and listening (meditation).

- Surrender to God and become humble. This means giving up some of your will (ego) in order to acknowledge God's superiority. It means allowing God to guide you from God's point of greater wisdom—"thy will be done."

- Give credit where credit is due. Be grateful to this "higher power" when you start to feel more peaceful, serene, and confident.

- If the benefits of spirituality don't seem readily apparent, don't lose hope. Some people have instantaneous spiritual awakenings but most of us grow into spirituality.

- To keep your faith strong, incorporate some spiritual exercises or disciplines into your life.

- Imagination and personification can enhance and maintain your spirituality. God is spirit, but I can give God human form and imagine that he or she is:
  - Protecting me
  - Walking with me
  - Holding me
  - Talking to me
  - Sharing my anger and frustrations
  - Giving me strength
  - Helping me let go of my anger

- Helping me forgive my persecutors
- Helping me look at others through his or her eyes
- Loving me unconditionally
- Helping me "accept what I cannot change" and change what should be changed.

• If all else fails, ask (pray) for willingness to know God and then build on that. Leave no stone unturned, and remember that "ask and it will be given to you; seek and you will find." Luke 11:9

Kathy

It was not easy for Kathy to totally accept spirituality or the concept of God. When she was young she stopped believing that God cared about her because he (or she) didn't seem to be answering her prayers. Then, when she was older, Kathy became an agnostic. She didn't believe we could prove God existed, so she thought why bother with the whole issue at all. Of course, sometimes she would acknowledge God as the power behind creation, but she could not see God as a source of love and power, or a spiritual being with whom she could interact. Surely, she thought, if God had been around at some point he had abandoned us.

In recovery, Kathy once again thought about God after she started going to 12-step meetings. The pain in her life had begun to subside and she felt as if she had been raised to a new level of consciousness. She didn't know why, or how it had happened, but she was suddenly filled with hope about the future, and for some reason she intuitively connected this with God. She somehow knew that God was a strong force behind her recovery.

Kathy also felt a deep urgency to become a better person, to pull herself out of the pit she had fallen into because of her addiction to love. She no longer felt that she was fine and that the rest of the world needed improving. Now, somehow, she knew that *she* was the one who had to change. She decided that this newfound hope and willingness to change was a gift from a benevolent force in the universe.

Kathy's newly acquired spirituality seemed both strange and fascinating at the same time. However, more than that, it piqued her curiosity and prompted her to seek out the source of all this benevolence. She wanted to say "thank you," and she wanted more. To find God, and to enhance her spirituality, Kathy went to the library to do some research. She didn't want to go to church because she wasn't interested in religion. She just wanted to know more about God.

Reading about spirituality was very enlightening, and it helped Kathy understand that she was not the only person seeking answers to questions about God. It became apparent to Kathy through her reading that many people have come to believe in God, including some of the greatest thinkers who have ever lived.

Feeling that she was in good company with regard to her spiritual quest, Kathy suddenly felt relieved of her hesitancy and embarrassment. This allowed her tender feelings for God to grow and bear fruit. Then, shortly thereafter, she had a wonderful experience. She was sitting in her kitchen. Everything was clean and bright. Her curtains were drawn and the sunlight poured through the window. Kathy was thinking about God and then suddenly a feeling of well-being took over her consciousness. She felt peaceful and content. All of her fears disappeared. She felt as if everything in the universe was in order. She just suddenly knew that even the chaos of this world was part of God's plan, and that everything was being taken care of. This serenity and trust was so exhilarating that Kathy felt overwhelmed and grateful. She closed her eyes and basked in the warmth of the sun and the "peace of God which passes all understanding." (Phil 4:7)

To Kathy, this spiritual experience was further evidence that God was real and that he or she loved her. Yet, for awhile it still seemed a bit disconcerting for Kathy to feel all of this growing tenderness for an invisible spirit. All of her life she had known what it felt like to fall in love with a person, but falling in love with God was something else. However, despite her trepidation, Kathy knew what was happening to her was wonderful, and she knew it was an experience to be cherished, not ignored. Like C.S. Lewis, she had been "surprised by joy."

To hold onto this new conscious contact with God, Kathy began to talk to Him/Her as one might talk to a close friend. Kathy did not really believe in petitioning God through prayer, so she just chatted away with an image of God that she created in her mind. She talked about her fears and her dreams. She talked about every subject under the sun. She said "good morning" and she said "goodnight." She said "thank you" for her newfound serenity. She just talked and talked until she really felt close to this power greater than herself. She also imagined herself as a little child being held and comforted by God. Everywhere she went, God went with her.

Of course, to Kathy, this budding friendship with God was quite exciting. Since she was a compulsive talker, having a non-stop conversation with an invisible friend was really a lot of fun. Then, one day Kathy had another spiritual experience. She was looking at herself in the mirror and feeling horrible about her body. She had never liked the way she looked. Then suddenly, she felt overwhelmed with a feeling of being loved and accepted. This feeling was so powerful that Kathy started to cry. Then she found herself sobbing and saying to God out loud, "You really don't care what I look like, do you? You really do love me just the way I am." Then Kathy sensed in a deep way God's unconditional love for her, and she was overwhelmed that God's love went beyond an appraisal of her physical appearance—that it was unconditional.

When Kathy stepped away from the mirror, she was still crying. She thought about how long she had waited for this type of acceptance and unconditional love. She thought about how she had looked for it from everyone she had ever loved and never found it. Now, finally, it had come from an unexpected source—from God and from within.

God's unconditional love validated Kathy. This validation

made up for the experience of being rejected by her parents when she was a child.

After learning that she was lovable, Kathy was able to learn how to love herself. As her self-esteem rose, she was able, for the first time in her life, to experience loving her family and community. This helped dissipate her obsession with romantic love.

Today, romantic love is still important to Kathy, but not important enough to obsess about. Romantic love is just the icing on the cake, and if necessary Kathy knows she can live without it. Furthermore, she has come to realize that her spirituality is the energy that pushes her forward in recovery. It is the source of her willingness to change and grow; it is the strength that keeps her going; it is the gift of transformation from a power greater than herself that can release her from the bondage of addiction.

CHRISTIAN IDEALS

You shall love your neighbor as yourself.

MATTHEW 22:38

Recovering love addicts who believe strongly in Christian ideals are often confused. They want to know if recovery means disowning such Christian concepts as sacrifice, unselfishness, dying to self, loving thy neighbor, putting yourself last, laying down your life, and staying married "as long as you both shall live." They also find that some Christian ideals are hard to understand. At first glance, they seem contradictory, confusing, or inconsistent with the concepts of recovery from addiction to love. Because of this, some recovering love addicts are tempted to abandon Christianity altogether. However, it doesn't have to be this way. Christian love addicts just need to be willing to sort the wheat from the chaff—to look more deeply into the meaning of Christian ideals and to make personal decisions about how to integrate them into their intimate relationships.

One of the most common mistakes love addicts make is to confuse Christian love with romantic love. Christian love, what Kierkegaard calls "eternal" love, is the love of God, ourselves, and our neighbor. This love operates under its own principles or laws. It is of God. It is unconditional. It is forever. It causes no pain, but can only fulfill us. When given away it comes back to us, somewhere along the way. Romantic love operates from a different set of laws or principles. It is object-oriented or based on "passionate preference" (attraction). It promises "forever" but rarely delivers. It can be euphoric, but it can also turn to hate; and for all the pleasure it brings, it also fosters suspicion, jealousy, despair and anxiety.

When love addicts do not understand the difference between these two forms of love, they often try to use spiritual love to promote romantic love. For instance, St. Francis of Assisi said that "it is in giving that we receive." This implies that if we give love we will receive love in return. This is true. The Christian love we give away does come back to us, not necessarily from the people we give it to or at the exact time we want it to be returned, but eventually it does come back to us through other people we meet along the path of life and from God. However, this spiritual principle of giving love to receive love does not work with romantic love. When love addicts don't understand this, they fall in love with someone who does not return their affection and suffer for a long period of time hoping that the spiritual principle of giving love to receive love will begin to work its magic and their faithfulness will be rewarded. Also, relationship addicts will take care of their partner only to find themselves fostering more contempt than love or gratitude. They see as much "biting the hand that feeds them" as they see love begetting love. This is because giving love to receive love does not work with romantic love. Romantic love requires attraction or passion, and spiritual love cannot make this happen. It just has to happen on its own.

Christianity also teaches us the concept of "dying to self"

or being unselfish. To many people this sounds like an order to abandon themselves in order to focus on meeting the needs of others. Many Christians recovering from their addiction to love struggle with this concept of "dying to self." They don't want to ignore it, and yet it seems contradictory to their attempt to build up their self-esteem. I usually tell these recovering love addicts that when asked by a scribe to proclaim God's *most important* commandment, Christ replied "You shall love the Lord your God with all your heart, and with all your soul, and with all your mind. This is the great and first commandment. And the second is like it. You shall love your neighbor *as* yourself." (Matthew 22:38-39). Note that this commandment does not say to love yourself less than your neighbor, but to love others *as much as* you love yourself. This implies that love for others should be in balance with self-love. Based on this, the most important commandment, I believe that total self-abandonment is only for those who aspire to sainthood; and for the rest of us who are not destined for this, it is all right to understand the Christian tenet of "dying to self" as a guideline for people who are in the habit of putting themselves above others—people with inflated egos whose self-centeredness has shut out God as well as others. For such people, "dying to self" is a good idea, if it is taken to mean moving away from total self-absorption.

Christian love addicts must understand that there is both a negative and positive aspect to selfishness. The positive part allows them to love, cherish and take care of themselves; to have self-esteem. The negative side of selfishness puts their needs ahead of others *at all times*. Christian love addicts in recovery must learn to enhance the positive side of selfishness and put the negative side into perspective. They can be unselfish when it is appropriate to do so, and they take care of themselves when that is appropriate.

Love addicts like to believe that when they make sacrifices they are being unselfish. Well, sometimes they are and sometimes they aren't. To tell the difference, recovering love addicts must learn to look at their motives for making sacrifices, because the act of being unselfish is not as important as the spiritual condition of the giver. Unhealthy motives include attempts to buy love, bolster insecurity, dissipate guilt, or abate fear. Healthy motives include love and kindness—feelings that originate from self-esteem and spill over into the lives of others.

How do you sort out healthy motivations from unhealthy ones? This process requires honesty and an insight into the addictive personality. Such perception is difficult, if not impossible, if love addicts are still clinging to distorted values, thoughts and behavior. However, after recovery has begun, an honest look into one's motivation can help put things into perspective.

Many love addicts read passages in the Bible about suffering, and they apply this to their marriage or romantic relationship. "Love bears all things...endures all things." (1 Cor 13:7) When they are abused they feel martyred, but they accept their punishment in the name of love. These recovering love addicts are confused. They are confusing accepting hardship with seeking it out. Jean-Pierre de Caussade makes this distinction in his book *Abandonment to Divine Providence*. He says a good Christian "...accepts cheerfully all the troubles they meet and submit to God's will in all that they have to do or suffer, *without in any way seeking out trouble for themselves*." It is true that if you are in a relationship you must sometimes endure hardship. For instance, if your partner gets ill you will have to endure hard times and make sacrifices. However, this sort of suffering is different from allowing yourself to be beaten up or trying to live with an alcoholic who is incapable of participating in a loving partnership. In recovery, Christian love addicts need to understand this. They must avoid martyring themselves in a relationship and thinking that this is the Christian thing to do.

One of the most difficult Christian ideals to clarify for recovering love addicts is Christ's suggestion that in a marriage "the two shall become one." (Mark 10:8) The King James version uses the phrase "one flesh." Does this mean that we are to have no personality boundaries? Does this mean we must give up our individuality in order to be in a relationship? I don't think so. I believe that Christ is just making the point that a marriage should be a *team* effort. A team is made up of individuals working together for a common goal.

Being a team does not necessarily require the fusion of both partners. Nor does it require that one partner abandon herself to become an imitation of the other. It just means that both partners share their uniqueness with each other. They work, share, love, and grow together (perhaps they serve God together), but they retain their sense of self. They each continue being the child of God they were created to be while joining forces with another individual.

CAN AN ADDICTIVE RELATIONSHIP BE SAVED?

When you keep wishing and hoping he will change.

ROBIN NORWOOD
in *Women Who Love Too Much*

Many recovering love addicts want to know if an addictive relationship can be repaired or saved. This is a good question, and the answer is that some relationships can be saved and others can't.

Relationships become addictive when obsession and an unhealthy dependency are present. If the love addict stops obsessing and being too dependent on his or her partner, sometimes the relationship can be salvaged. However, usually a love addict has selected an unhealthy partner who also has an addiction of his or her own, and unless this person also gets into recovery the relationship cannot survive. Creating a healthy relationship requires two healthy people working toward a common goal. This goal is their own personal growth which contributes to the growth of the relationship.

Saving an addictive relationship is a difficult task. It requires a lot of patience. At the same time, there is a fine line between being patient and "loving too much." Not all recovering love addicts can walk this fine line.

ENDING A RELATIONSHIP WHEN IT IS NECESSARY

Success lies in being able to retreat at the right moment and in the right manner. The success is made possible by the fact that the retreat is not the forced flight of a weak person but the voluntary withdrawal of a strong one.

The I Ching or Book of Changes

Now and then, no matter how hard you try to turn an addictive relationship into a healthy one, you have to admit defeat and call it quits. The following suggestions may prove helpful if this is the case.

SUGGESTIONS

- Face your fears:
  - Fear of loneliness:
    I'll never find anyone else
    I can't make it alone
    I'll be alone forever
    Being alone is terrifying

- Financial fears:
    I can't take care of the kids alone
    I won't find a job
- Fear of being a failure:
    Leaving is failing
    I can't mess up another relationship
- Fear of cultural pressures:
    I'm a Christian. I can't get divorced.
- Fear mixed with guilt:
    I am abandoning him
    She can't make it without me
    I put up with him this long, why stop now
    I can't bear to hurt her
    I owe her for taking care of me
- Fear of reprisal:
    She won't let me go without a fight
    He will hurt me
    He will hurt the kids
    She will tell our friends lies
    He won't give me financial support
- Fear of suffering:
    I can't stand the pain

- Plan ahead:
  - Find emotional support (group/therapist)
  - Be practical. Make plans regarding jobs and housing.

- Leave:
  - How you leave depends on your situation and what works. Some people, for the sake of their sanity or because they have children with their partner, have to ease off. Some people can only make the separation if

they never see the person again. Some people can become friends, but only after the grief is over.

- Facing withdrawal after you have left:
  - Make a list of everything that supports your decision to leave. Re-read it when you are tempted to go running back.
  - Write in your journal. Express your feelings.
  - Stay close to your friends:

    To get advice

    To remind you of why you left

    For companionship

    For reassurance

    To listen to you
  - Separate thoughts from feelings. Change "desperate" thoughts to "manageable" thoughts and let go of thoughts that cause fear.
  - Deal with depression:

    Depression will be part of your withdrawal symptoms. Emotional depression is experienced when love addicts are overloaded with anger, frustration, anxiety and fear. It is experienced midway between letting go and real acceptance. That is, when love addicts have let go in their conscious state (mind) but are still holding on in their unconscious state (heart), they are apt to become depressed. This is natural and part of the process of moving on. Usually their inner child is taking over at this point and they are feeling "blue" because their need to attach with someone has been thwarted once again. And they are also afraid. They feel abandoned and/or rejected. They feel alone and cut adrift from everybody and everything, so they shut down. Remember that depression is often a secondary emotional state caused by the primary emotions of anger, fear, and hopelessness. Work on letting go of these feelings and the depression will lift.

What to do about depression:

Check with your doctor to see if you have a phys-iological problem. But be careful; many doctors are too eager to mask the symptoms of depression with drugs and sometimes it is better to deal with your feelings outright.

Read about depression. (Try David Burn's *Feeling Good: The New Mood Therapy*.)

Look more closely at the source of your depression. Is it just the ending of the relationship or did that loss trigger other feelings left over from the past?

Try to face your depression. By this I mean don't worry about it. Just flow with it until it passes.

Take good care of your health.

Be especially nice to yourself.

Stop blaming yourself.

Stop comparing yourself to others.

Don't look at this as failure.

Don't shut down and isolate.

Talk about your feelings.

Try to keep busy.

Keep your spiritual program strong.

Do something new.

Look at the bright side.

Think about what you have learned and what changes you will be making in the future.

- Resistance from your partner: Some partners cry, plead, and promise to change. Some partners threaten to hurt themselves. They make a suicide attempt, or they abuse drugs and/or alcohol. Some partners get violent or at least threaten you with bodily harm. Some partners withhold financial resources such ar alimony or child support. All of this is designed to get you to feel sorry for them and change your mind about leaving.

Despite resistance from your partner, try to hang in there. This may mean changing your phone number or getting a restraining order, but if it is time to move on you have to be willing to go to any length.

BEING SINGLE

Is It Really a Fate Worse Than Death?

Naturally. How one hates to think of oneself alone. How one avoids it. It seems to imply rejection or unpopularity. An early wall-flower panic still clings to the world. One will be left, one fears, sitting in a straight-backed chair alone, while the popular girls are already chosen and spinning around the dance floor with their hot-palmed partners. We seem so frightened today of being alone that we never let it happen…When the noise stops there is no inner music to take its place. We must re-learn to be alone.

ANN MORROW LINDBERGH
in *Women and Solitude*

For most love addicts, being single is something to be avoided at all costs. They cling to the idea that being in an intimate relationship is more important than life itself. Being single almost terrifies them because they equate it with agonizing loneliness and deprivation.

Love addicts in recovery must have a change of attitude about being single. They must accept the fact that being without a partner is not a fate worse than death. It has its advantages and disadvantages, just like a relationship, and there are times in life when it is inevitable.

Having a positive attitude about being single accomplishes several things. First of all, it allows love addicts to be comfortable when there is no one "special" in their lives. Being alone is not painful for them; it is a time of cherished solitude. Also, by accepting their single status gracefully, love addicts in recovery experience an inner confidence that actually goes a long way toward attracting the kind of emotionally stable people they might like to become involved with. Furthermore, being content to be single allows recovering love addicts to be discriminating in their choice of a partner. They can afford to be choosey, for the first time in their lives, because being in a relationship is just an option, not a life or death matter. Finally, being satisfied with their single status makes it easier for love addicts to be patient. There is no deadline to meet, no need to frantically pursue a potential partner as if time were running out.

If they are progressing in their recovery, love addicts should be experiencing a boost in self-esteem. This, along with spirituality, should reduce their dislike and fear of being alone, and make it easier for them to adopt a positive attitude about not having a partner. This is the trick. There must be a change in attitude or values. This does not mean recovering love addicts have to be overjoyed about being single. I am talking about acceptance, not overwhelming enthusiasm. It is just important to consistently look at the bright side until this positive attitude is well entrenched in the love addict's psyche. This will then subdue the voice that wails, "You're nobody till somebody loves you."

Please note that I am not trying to establish a case for or against being single. It is just important for recovering love addicts to be comfortable with both situations. Then they can flow contentedly with life instead of frantically trying to control it.

VII.

STARTING
OVER
AGAIN

Sing and dance together and be joyous, but let each one of you be alone, even as the strings of a lute are alone, but though they quiver with the same music…and stand together, yet not too near together, for the pillars of the temple stand apart, and the oak tree and the cypress grow not in each other's shadow.

KAHIL GIBRAN in *The Prophet*

Personality Types That Trigger Addictive Behavior

*Every thought, every moment, every day is a
choice; choose well.*

AUTHOR UNKNOWN

Love addicts in recovery should take note of the fact that certain types of people can trigger their addiction. With some love addicts it is the person who needs help, someone who brings out their caretaking instincts. Other love addicts must watch out for the controlling and dominant person who makes it easier for them to avoid taking responsibility for themselves. Still other love addicts always seem to get hooked on the artificially beautiful or handsome person—someone who has no inner beauty. And finally, most love addicts need to watch out for someone who reminds them of one of their parents if that parent was unhealthy—*my heart belongs to Daddy* or *I want a girl just like the girl who married dear old dad.*

The worst personality type for love addicts is the narcissist. Narcissists are unavailable because they are terrified of engulfment. Pia Mellody in her book, *Facing Love Addiction*, calls

these people "avoidance addicts." Because they are unavailable, narcissists always trigger the love addict's fear of abandonment which then triggers the love addict's addictive
thinking and behavior. On the following two pages I have listed the traits of both the love addict and the narcissist. These
two types of people bring out the worst in each other.

THE LOVE ADDICT

The Person Who Fears Abandonment

- Has a fear of being alone
- Has a fear of being independent
- Bonds too quickly
- Bonds too tightly
- Gets addicted to people and relationships
- Clings to people—can't let go
- When someone needs "space" they feel rejected
- Is caught up in the lives of others
- Is a caretaker
- Copes with abuse
- Has no sexual boundaries
- Walks on eggshells around his or her partner
- Goes along with other people's plans
- Needs constant reassurance that his or her partner
  is there
- Protects other people from negative feelings
- Is reassured by things going well and then asks for more

THE NARCISSIST*

The Person Who Fears Engulfment

- Fears losing his or her identity
- Fears dependency/avoids bonding
- Creates rigid personality boundaries (won't let people in)
- Is sensitive to everything that leads to bonding
- Loses interest in sex that leads to bonding
- Seduces and withholds to avoid bonding
- Minimizes feelings that lead to bonding
- Gets nervous when things go well or bonding occurs
- Picks fights and creates uproars to avoid bonding
- Wants more space or has to run
- Can't make commitment
- Is indifferent to others
- Feels entitled to be taken care of (his or her way)
- Won't put up with discomfort
- Has complete control of the schedule
- Says to partner "Just stay put while I come and go"

THE FEAR OF INTIMACY: UNDERLYING THE YEARNING TO LOVE AND BE LOVED

Robin Norwood, in *Women Who Love Too Much*, says that some women cling to men who are emotionally unavailable because unconsciously they are afraid of real intimacy. In

*Adapted from "How to be an Adult" by David Richo

other words, underlying their hope that an unloving man will become more loving, is their fear that he will.

Usually, love addicts are not aware of their unconscious fear of intimacy because they are overwhelmed by the conscious emotions triggered by their obsession. They feel a tremendous attraction to someone and this suppresses their unacknowledged fear.

One symptom of this underlying fear of intimacy is an aversion to nice people. Love addicts in recovery may tell themselves (and others) that they are looking for someone nice, but when they meet such a person they feel uncomfortable or unstimulated—there will be no overwhelming attraction or excitement in the initial stages of the relationship. The "pull" or the "draw" to be with this person will not be there.

This is sad but it does not have to be a permanent problem. To move beyond this stage of recovery, love addicts must learn to see the value of a healthy relationship with a nice person, even if that person seems unstimulating at first or the relationship lacks the melodrama of an addictive relationship. Then, when recovering love addicts start getting to know healthy, available, loving partners, they can begin to face their fear of intimacy.

In my opinion, the best way to handle the fear of intimacy underlying our yearning to be loved, is to face it. This involves acknowledging the feelings of anxiety, but keeping a cool head. It means sorting out legitimate feelings of hesitancy (that act as a warning sign of something unhealthy) from feelings of anxiety that stem from the fear of intimacy.

SUGGESTIONS

- Be honest with yourself about your perception of love. Do you confuse the adrenalin rush of passion or a cha otic relationship with love? Is pain the measure of your love? (Do you tell yourself that if you weren't in love you wouldn't be hurting so much?) Have you become

crisis-oriented after all these years of living with tumul-
tuous, unhealthy relationships?

- Re-evaluate your feelings about "boredom." Why does it
  seem like a "fate worse than death?" Do you confuse
  being comfortable and relaxed with being bored? Can
  you find other ways to experience excitement besides
  addictive relationships?

- When you get involved with someone, evaluate the
  relationship using criteria other than just the level of
  your sexual attraction. The importance you give to
  being attracted to someone is not a good way to measure
  the quality of a relationship. (You are too used to being
  attracted to the wrong types.) Ask yourself if the person
  you are with is patient, trustworthy, considerate, understanding, generous, shares your values, has some interests similar to yours, is concerned about your needs,
  fights fair, and is ready to consider a commitment.

- Be in the company of nice people so that you can get
  used to it. This can prepare you for a more serious relationship with someone nice later on. (A really healthy
  union may start out romantic, but in the final analysis it
  will have all the components of a healthy friendship.
  Love addicts need to find out what these components are.)

- Be patient with yourself. You are doing positive things
  for a change and in many respects you are like a young
  adolescent starting all over again. Now that you aren't
  controlling everything and everyone anymore, you are
  apt to be very frightened.

- Get outside of your comfort zone. Walk in a strange land
  until your fears subside and you can see the beauty of
  your surroundings. "The only way out is through." *Robin
  Norwood*

HIDDEN SIGNALS

Love addicts always start out looking for someone to love, and end up with an unloving partner instead. This is not just an accident. This is the result of certain behavior patterns exhibited by love addicts during the selection process. I call these behavior patterns "signals," and in my opinion they will determine (1) what sort of person the love addict ends up with, and (2) what the course of the relationship will be.

To illustrate my point, and to demonstrate what *not to do* during the selection process, I have written a dialogue between a love addict (Wanda) and a man she has recently met (John). Can you pick up on the signals that Wanda gives out about her hunger for love, impatience, and need to control? (Note: Wanda could just as easily be a man. Men are love addicts too.)

WEDNESDAY:

John and Wanda run into each other at the local shopping mall.

Wanda: Hi John, how have you been? I haven't seen you around lately.

John: Oh, I'm fine, just busy that's all. What's new with you?

Wanda: Not a lot, the same old boring life.

John: That's too bad, but I'm sure things will pick up.

Wanda: I hope so, but this seems to be the story of my life.

John: (*In a hurry to get going*) Well, it's been nice running into you Wanda.

Wanda: You're always on the run John, let's get together sometime for coffee so we can really catch up.

John: Sure, that sounds great.

Wanda: What about Friday?

John: (*Hesitating*) Well sure.

Wanda: Great, where shall we meet?

John: What's good for you?

Wanda: Oh anything is ok. Name the time and place.

John: Well, I'll tell you what, how about meeting me at Carrows restaurant about 6:00.

Wanda: Wonderful. I'll be looking forward to it. Maybe we can even catch a movie.

THURSDAY:

Right after work Wanda bolts over to a department store to find a stunning new outfit. She wants to look just right. When she gets home she calls all her friends to tell them the "good news," and as she drifts off to sleep she fantasizes about how her date with John will turn out and what it might lead to.

FRIDAY:

Wanda is dressed to kill and arrives at the coffee shop early. John shows up about 20 minutes late, dressed more casually. Wanda has been worried (afraid that he won't show up) and when he sits down she looks "too" relieved. Trying to hide this, she flashes him a nervous smile.

John: Sorry I'm late. I forgot the time.

Wanda: Oh don't worry about it. I just hope you're alright. I was concerned about you.

John is a little surprised at how concerned Wanda is.

John: Oh, I'm fine. I just had some other things on my mind and forgot for a moment that we were going to get together. Sometimes I wish I had a secretary to organize my life.

Wanda: Oh, I'm a great organizer. Let me know if I can help you with anything.

John looks surprised.

John: Sure.

Wanda: Well now that you're here, tell me how you've been since Wednesday.

John: Fine, just busy that's all. Between work, jogging and my friends time flies by.

For the next hour John tries to talk about casual things, while Wanda talks on a more serious note, telling him her life story (including her failures in relationships).

Wanda: Well, how about that movie we talked about?

John: Sure. What would you like to see?

Wanda: Oh anything, I don't really have a preference. What would you like to see?

John: Well I heard that *Rambo* is pretty good. Is that too heavy for you?

Wanda: (*Lying*) Oh no, that sounds great. And by the way, it will be my treat since the movie was my idea.

AFTER THE MOVIE:

John: That was great. Life in a nutshell. That Stallone is really a man's man.

Wanda: It was exciting alright. I'm glad you enjoyed it. It really glorifies violence though. Sometimes I wonder if the media goes a little too far.

John: I don't think so. This is life as it really is.

Wanda: But there is another side to life.

John: I guess, but this is where it's really at. Force, aggression, defending yourself, taking the hard line. It's a dog-eat-dog world out there.

Wanda: I guess you're right.

WALKING WANDA BACK TO HER CAR:

John: Well, I had a great time Wanda. Thanks for suggesting it.

Wanda: Me too. We'll have to do this again soon. I'm free anytime.

John: Ok, I'll give you a ring.

(John does not ask for her phone number even though he doesn't have it.)

Wanda: Great, but don't you want my phone number?

John: Oh yeah, I forgot I don't have it.

(He takes her number)

Wanda: Thanks for a great time. I haven't had so much fun in ages. Take care of yourself. I don't want anything to happen to you.

John: Sure—Well, see you later.

Wanda: I really hope so, I'll be waiting for your call. I get home about 6:00 but you can call as late as you want.

Giving Out Signals *or* What Not to Do on Your First Date

- By saying "*My life is boring…I guess that's the story of my life,*" Wanda is revealing her fatalist or victim mentality. The hidden message here is "I need someone to fix my boring life—you."

- By saying *"Anything you want..."* Wanda is revealing her willingness to please by being over-accommodating. If this becomes a pattern, Wanda is also revealing that she has no personality of her own or is at least willing to lose her personality in his.

- By saying *"How about Friday... Maybe we can even catch a movie..."* Wanda is revealing her impatience, and need to control. She wants too much too soon, and by being so pushy she is giving out signals of insecurity and neediness.

- Wanda is overdressed, or dressed too perfectly. Wanting to look nice on a first date is normal, but you can go too far or fuss too much, thus revealing how anxious you are to impress someone. This is part of image management and control. Be conscientious about your appearance, not dressed to kill.

- By saying *"Don't worry about being late...I was concerned about you..."* Wanda is revealing once again how much energy and concern she has put into this date. She expresses a sense of urgency that can be readily picked up. The message here is, "This date is important to me —life or death." This concern about John might be appropriate later on, but it is out of place on a first date. Wanda should be more concerned about establishing how she feels about punctuality (either pro or con).

- When Wanda says *"I'm a great organizer..."* she is trying to impress John and at the same time she is being too helpful, too soon. She is trying to impress John with her skills and eager to start "earning" his attention. Wanda has all the earmarks of a rescuer, provider, caretaker and/or martyr.

- Wanda tells John her life story. Wanda is once again revealing her impatience or need to control.

- If she has a sordid story, she is anxious to get it out of the way to see if there is going to be a problem in this area. She wants to get the rejection over with, if there is going to be any. (Fear of rejection often appears as early as the first date.) Unfortunately, John may be overwhelmed by her "confession" if he has not had time to develop positive feelings for her and therefore be motivated to put aside his misgivings about her past life.

- If Wanda has a sad story, then her intent here is to manipulate John into feeling sorry for her. This is controlling and it doesn't work. His sympathy (if he has any) will not blossom into love, as Wanda hopes.

- If Wanda has had a fascinating or successful life, then her intent here is to impress John. John may see right through Wanda (noting her exaggerated need to impress him), or he may misunderstand her intention and just feel she is bragging or being egocentric. This is not to say that a woman should hide her success story, just that her achievements should speak for themselves as the relationship unfolds.

Whatever the story of your life, the details should be revealed slowly and naturally as the relationship progresses (not on the first date), and not in order to manipulate the person you are sharing your story with.

- By lying and saying *"Oh no, that sounds great..."* Wanda is being dishonest. Once again, this is image management, or an attempt to control how John sees her. This, in turn, is motivated by Wanda's fear of rejection. It would be better for Wanda to let John respond to who she really is by revealing her tastes and personality. She can go to the *Rambo* movie, but she should not lie and pretend that she likes that type of movie. Dishonesty is a bad foundation—or no foundation at all—on which to build a relationship.

- *"And by the way, it will be my treat since the movie was my idea."* In this modern age it is not necessarily inappropriate to treat a man to a night out; however, this is best left to emotionally healthy and confident women. Insecure, needy women like Wanda are revealing too much when they offer to pay before the date has even taken place. The hidden signal here is "I really want to go out with you at any cost, don't back down because of money."

- By saying *"I guess you're right…"* Wanda is capitulating to John's assessment of the Rambo movie. She is being dishonest once again for the same reasons mentioned above (image management and fear of rejection). It would be better for Wanda to be true to her opinion and just "agree to disagree" with John. If John is secure and emotionally healthy, he will respect Wanda for this and gain some important information about her values and point of view. If he doesn't like who she is, then it is better to find out now before things go any further.

- *"Great, but don't you want my phone number…?"* Wanda may or may not be pushing too hard here. Maybe John is so excited about seeing her that he honestly did forget to ask for her phone number. However, it's more likely that he is graciously trying to back out of calling her. Even if he is *not* trying to back out, in offering John her phone number Wanda is not allowing him to be responsible for his own carelessness. She is being the responsible one and this reveals a lot about the position she will be willing to take if the relationship gets off the ground. In the final analysis, it is not so much that it's inappropriate for Wanda to offer John her phone number, but that in the context of the rest of their conversation it may very well be just another hidden message.

- By saying *"I haven't had so much fun in ages…"* Wanda is making it very clear that she can't have fun on her own—that it is up to John, or somebody like him, to bring fun into her life. Or she may be revealing that no one else is interested in her right now, and John may wonder why.

- "*Take care of yourself, I don't want anything to happen to you.*" This is a considerate remark coming from an emotionally healthy, confident woman. But coming from Wanda, and coupled with the other things she has said, this concern reveals once again a kind of "too much too soon" attitude on Wanda's part. It would be better for Wanda just to say something like, "Good-bye and take care."

- When Wanda says "*I'm free anytime...I'll be waiting for your call...You can call as late as you want...*" she is really being obvious. She wants to see John again and she makes it clear that she is available. No mystery here, nothing to get John excited about the challenge of winning over this nice woman. Wanda is once again revealing how anxious she is and how much emotional energy she has invested in the outcome of this date. A really sharp man could see that Wanda is already "future tripping," which is one step removed from having expectations and making plans. This can be intimidating or a turn-off on the first date. Also, something about the way Wanda phrases her remarks makes it seem that she *is* *assuming* John is going to call her. Her need to make her fantasies come true may be revealing itself at this point in a false sense of confidence that he *will* call. Maybe in her mind they are halfway to the altar by now. Or Wanda may even be using a subtle form of mind control to convince John that he is expected to call. Anything is possible when you are insecure and hungry for love.

PICKING UP THE SIGNALS

Originally, John has seen this evening as a casual encounter. Now he begins to reflect for a minute about whether or not he wants to pick up on Wanda's encouragement to get together again.

At this point, if John is an emotionally healthy person (and not too egocentric to be blinded by all this attention), he is very wary of Wanda and will probably never call her. Healthy men pick up on the signals coming from a needy woman, and this intimidates them tremendously. If John is perceptive, he has noticed that Wanda is over-anxious, impatient, too accommodating, too eager to please, too needy, too controlling or pushy, and too willing to compromise her values and tastes or at least unwilling to reveal her true personality. This bothers him. If he can't read between the lines, he will just see Wanda as too pushy one minute and then too accommodating or wishy-washy the next. He won't analyze it, he just won't like it.

If John is emotionally unhealthy, or terribly egocentric, he will probably be flattered by Wanda's attentions and want to see her again. His encouragement will draw Wanda into an addictive relationship very quickly. He may also become addicted himself, if he is looking for a "clinging vine" who will cater to his every need.

If John is the type of person who uses women, he will realize right away (from experience) that Wanda has all the earmarks of being a caretaker. He doesn't really analyze the situation, or understand the phenomenon; he just knows that she is a possible gold mine for him if he wants to be taken care of, have his way all the time, or just have all the comforts of a relationship without having to get close or give any love in return.

If John is a misogynist (woman hater) he will zero in on Wanda. He will start to ask her out and be very charming until the relationship is established and he feels free to expose his moody, angry side.

VIII.

CREATING
LOVING AND
FULFILLING
RELATIONSHIPS

Throughout history, in all cultures, the relationship of man and woman has been regarded as sacred, not just something pleasurable or exciting, but a microcosm of the dynamic interplay of larger energies in the cosmos.

JOHN WELWOOD
in *The Challenge of the Heart*

THE INGREDIENTS OF A HEALTHY RELATIONSHIP

If you have recovered (to one degree or another) from addiction to love, you are ready to create a loving and fulfilling relationship. Creating a relationship is like baking a cake. You must have the right ingredients, in the right amount (not too much and not too little) and you must put them together in the right order. The ingredients of a healthy relationship are as follows:

• *Honesty* that engenders trust—this is mandatory.

• *Readiness* for a relationship is also very important.

• The *willingness to negotiate* or compromise is part of a healthy relationship.

• *Self-awareness*—this means both partners knowing who they are and what they want.

• *Self-esteem* is mandatory in a healthy relationship—this means both partners feeling good about themselves.

• *Communication skills* are mandatory. This means:
  – Asking for what you want, but not being addicted to getting it.

143

- Fighting fair—this means expressing your opinion without attacking the other person.
- Reporting your feelings.
- Saying what you mean (not beating around the bush).
- Listening as well as talking.

• *Sexual compatibility* is important. This means similar values and preferences with regard to sexual issues.

• A *recognition* of the fact that there are 4 people in the relationship—*2 adults and 2 children* (1 inner child per adult). This means:

- That childhood wounds will probably be triggered and sensitivity strategies must be created.
- That rituals from your family of origin must be re-negotiated and new rituals created as a couple.
- That the wounded inner child must be kept in check. (In other words, love your inner child, but don't give him or her the keys to the car.)

• *Similar (but not necessarily identical) values* about such issues as money, religion, monogamy, and parenting. This avoids needless conflict. Still, you don't have to agree about everything—just what's important to you.

• *Patience* and *tolerance* are ingredients in a healthy relationship; but you should never tolerate abuse.

• *Acceptance* of the fact that there will be days in which your relationship seems very ordinary or even boring. Love addicts tend to have an "all or nothing" mentality. They either want a relationship to be exciting all the time, or they live with unbearable pain rather than move on. Healthy relationships are sometimes luke warm.

- The *willingness to substitute influencing for controlling* is important.
  - This means saying something once and then letting it go.
  - It also means being a role model instead of nagging someone to change.

- The *willingness to keep your personality boundaries* (even when you feel like losing yourself in the other person) is important. This is how we maintain our self-esteem.

- *Devotion* enhances a relationship. How can an intimate relationship feel good if both people aren't *special* to each other?

- *Quality time together* is important. At the same time, you want to set aside time for personal interests. Look for balance.

- *Knowing when to stay and when to leave* is important. This means staying when things are going well (and you feel like running), and being willing to let go of the relationship if it cannot be saved.

- *Compatibility* and "ease" in a relationship are important. Yet, at the same time, it must be understood that no relationship is perfect. (Compatibility comes from being alike or having a high tolerance for your partner's differences.)

- The *willingness to face your problems* (without over-reacting to them) is important.

- *Respect* and *admiration* can enhance a relationship, but there should also be an understanding that your partner will *not* always look good to you.

- *Reciprocity* (give and take) is mandatory in a healthy

relationship, but you should also be willing to make sacrifices now and then.

- Finally, it is important to have *realistic expectations* about how much of your happiness should come from the relationship—not too much and not too little.

THE PROGRESSION OF A HEALTHY RELATIONSHIP

Misses! the tale that I relate This lesson seems to carry—Choose not alone a proper mate, But a proper time to marry.

CHARLES CHURCHILL
in *Pairing Time Anticipated*

The proper progression of a relationship might vary from couple to couple but here are some guidelines:

- Before you get started:
  - Develop a fulfilling relationship with yourself before you attempt to have a romantic relationship.Romantic feelings can be like a tidal wave sweeping you out to sea if you are not securely tied to a relationship with yourself. *Many of you may want to be swept out to sea, but this is not really healthy; and sometimes it is even dangerous.*

- Selection is everything:
  - Take your time.
  - Do everything you can to keep from being blinded by your emotions.
  - Know what you *don't* want (people who trigger your dysfunctional behavior).

- Look for someone healthy, and observe them objectively before you plunge in.

- Look for someone who does not have to change very much too please you; but don't be *too* picky. Find the middle ground.

- Know what you *do* want. Make a list of the things that are mandatory and the things that are optional. Prioritize your list.

• Dating:
  - This is when you find out what this person is really like—any false fronts should crumble after a few dates.

  - Be yourself—you want someone to know who you really are.

  - Measure your compatibility during this time.

  - Establish trust.

  - Hold off on sex if it blinds you to what this person is really like, and keep a lid on any budding romantic feelings (you may feel them, but don't give them a lot of power by fantasizing too much).

  - Be willing to change your mind if you usually "cling" to unhealthy people and be willing to hang in there if you usually "run."

• Friendship:
  - See if you can relax and have fun together.

  - See if you can count on this person.

  - Continue to see if there is enough compatibility to sustain the relationship.

  - Build a strong foundation for a future romantic relationship.

• Courtship:
  - This is friendship combined with romance.

- Romantic feelings can now have a free reign—see if they mix well with the friendship.

- You can let romantic love blossom now—you don't have to put a lid on your feelings anymore.

- Now you can test your readiness for intimacy; this is usually the time when a fear of intimacy comes up— if you have any.

• Commitment:

- Now things are getting serious.

- Set ground rules for the relationship.

- Discuss things like:

  Fidelity

  Growing closer

  The future

  How much time you will have for each other

  ...anything that is important to you.

• Partnership (this used to be called marriage, but now the wedding ceremony is optional):

- During a partnership you should:

  Maintain what you have established up to now.

  Honor the values you have in common.

  Grow as a couple, as well as individuals.

  Get to really know each other and experience intimacy. (Intimacy comes from revealing yourself to a non-judgmental partner.)

• Switch:

- At any point in the progression of a relationship, one partner may experience a fear of intimacy and pull back. Don't panic. Give your partner some space. However, if he or she does not come around in a few weeks you should move on. (This is discussed more fully in A *Fine Romance* by Judith Sills.)

Now, I want to give you a word of encouragement and a warning. Intimate relationships are wonderful and something to aspire to. They can enhance your life in unbelievable ways. They can be very fulfilling and help you grow to your full potential. But always remember that they are a "want" not a "need." Your self-esteem should never depend on finding someone special.

Also, love (as attraction and desire) is not enough. Love that follows a careful selection, and is coupled with a willingness to work hard and extend yourself is also necessary.

Finally, you must not become slaves to the myth that preferential love will always span an entire lifetime. Only spiritual love lasts forever. Therefore, as *you* change, your relationship will change; and sometimes (but not always) it will fade away. You should not be discouraged by this. Change is part of life. It is what makes life interesting.

Kathy

As Kathy's recovery progressed she began to think about whether or not she wanted to be in a relationship. She was happy to be single, but she also saw the benefits of being in a loving relationship.

After talking it over with her support group and therapist, Kathy decided she did want to be with someone, so she began to socialize a little bit more than she had in early recovery. She also spent a lot of time doing her favorite exercise—hiking.

One beautiful afternoon Kathy was hiking in the Yosemite valley with a group of people in the Sierra Club. This is where she met Ted. He was a pleasant person and fun to be around. At the end of the trip Ted asked Kathy if he could call her. Kathy agreed and gave him her phone number.

A couple of weeks later Ted called Kathy and asked her out. He said he wanted to see a movie and was looking for a companion. Kathy accepted the invitation and a week later she and Ted went to the movie together. After this Ted called every couple of weeks and asked Kathy to join him on one outing after another. Each time she went with Ted, Kathy had a good time. She was also attracted to him but she didn't do anything about her budding romantic feelings.

As Kathy and Ted continued to see each other they found out they had a lot in common. They enjoyed several of the same activities and their values were similar. Ted had a stable career as a banker and he attended church regularly. Kathy had just started a new and exciting career, and went to another church across town. As Ted and Kathy talked about the things that were important to them, a bond began to build.

One day, Ted called Kathy and asked her if she wanted to get together on the weekend. Kathy agreed that this would be fun and asked Ted what activity he had in mind. Ted said "Kathy, I've reached that stage where I don't care what we do, I just enjoy your company. You're a good friend and I really care for you in a special way." Kathy was delighted because she felt the same way.

Kathy and Ted stayed friends for several months even after they both began to have romantic feelings toward each other. Then, when Ted finally announced that he was in love with Kathy, she was finally free to unleash the romantic feelings she had been holding back.

After this, Kathy and Ted started spending every weekend together. They both agreed that they would not date other people from this point on. Kathy was very happy. Time had proven that Ted was an honest and sincere person who would not trigger Kathy's addiction. Furthermore, he was attentive and gave as much in the relationship as she did.

As the time went by, Kathy and Ted decided they really wanted to make an even deeper commitment to each other, so they decided to get married. This was very frightening for

Kathy. She did not know if she was able to go this far. All of her life she had yearned for intimacy and yet now that she had it she was feeling ill at ease. Sometimes she felt a knot it her stomach and her sexual desire just disappeared. Sometimes she was so disconcerted that she picked on Ted by being over-ly critical. She felt as if she was sabotaging her chances for happiness.

Fortunately, with the help of her therapist, and support group, Kathy was able to ride out her misgivings. She knew she was just afraid of getting hurt again and was trying to avoid this stage of growth in her recovery. Knowing what was wrong helped ease her fear, and eventually she agreed to marry Ted. They had a simple ceremony on Valentine's day, and the last time I talked to Kathy she was happy to be married and grateful that she had come so far in recovery.

APPENDIX

WORKSHEET #1

Am I a Love Addict?

Answer questions 1-32 using the following point system:

Most of the time   = 2

Some of the time   = 1

Hardly ever   = 0

1. _____ I am very needy.

2. _____ I fall in love almost over night.

3. _____ When I fall in love, I obsess. I can't help myself.

4. _____ When I am looking for a relationship, I will get involved with almost anyone who shows any interest in me.

5. _____ I tend to smother my partners.

6. _____ I will hold onto a relationship no matter how unhealthy it is or what it costs.

7. _____ I always fall in love with the wrong people.

8. _____ I either trust the wrong person or I can't trust at all.

9. _____ When a relationship ends, I feel as if my life is over.

10. _____ When a relationship ends, I want to kill myself.

11. _____ I take on more than my share of responsibility for the survival of a relationship.

12. _____ I find myself loving people from afar.

13. _____ I really don't feel good about myself.

14. _____ I really don't know who I am.

15. _____ Sometimes I feel superior and other times I feel inferior. I rarely feel "just right."

16. _____ A lot of the time I feel alienated, as if I don't fit in.

17. _____ I can't stand being alone. I don't enjoy my own company.

18. _____ I am very lonely when I am not in a relationship.

19. _____ When one relationship ends, I get into another one as soon as possible.

20. _____ I am terrified of never finding someone special to love.

21. _____ In relationships, I don't know where my needs, wants, and values leave off and my partner's begins.

22. _____ I can't say "no" to my partner.

23. _____ I try hard to be who my partner wants me to be. I will do anything to please him or her.

24. _____ I have very few interests outside of my relationship.

25. _____ I will suffer rather than let go of a relationship.

26. _____ When I start to get involved with someone, I become terrified that he or she will do to me what others have done to me in the past.

27. _____ I am very controlling in relationships. This is the only way I can feel comfortable.

28._____ I do not know how to fight fairly. I attack people when they disagree with me or give them the silent treatment.

29._____ I am very sensitive. It really hurts my feelings when people criticize me.

30._____ I over-react to anything that feels like rejection.

31._____ I just know that a romantic relationship is going to fix everything that is wrong with my life.

32._____ I don't have any energy to make my life better.

SCORING:

0   You are *not* a love addict.

0-16 You are a *potential* love addict—be careful.

17-32 You *are* on the brink of becoming a love addict.

33-48 You *are* a love addict and should consider getting some help before things get any worse.

49-64 You *are* a full-blown love addict and should get into a recovery program right away.

WORKSHEET #2

An Inventory of My Unhealthy Relationships

Indicate the kinds of unhealthy relationships you have had. Make comments if you like.

• My partner was emotionally unavailable:

• My partner was a commitment phobic:

• I had an affair with a married person:

• My partner was irresponsible, selfish, and immature:

- My partner was abusive:

- My partner was addicted to something outside of the relationship:

- I was in love with a seductive withholder:

- I obsessed about someone from afar—the relationship was only in my head:

- My partner and I only had one good thing going for us:

- Is there a pattern?

- Have you ever had a *healthy* relationship?

- Do you realize that you chose these people?

- Do you realize that you can make wiser choices?

Take stock of everything you've written above. Think of constructive life changes you can make based on this information. By writing things down we are able to confront our problems in a more tangible and focused way and come up with insightful solutions.

WORKSHEET #3

Am I Ready for a Healthy Relationship?

Answer questions 1-42 using the following point system:

Most of the time   = 2

Some of the time   = 1

Hardly ever   = 0

1. _____ I know I am lovable despite my short-comings.

2. _____ I have self-discipline.

3. _____ I am honest.

4. _____ I am true to my values.

5. _____ I am responsible.

6. _____ I know myself—what my values are and what I want.

7. _____ I can talk about my feelings.

8. _____ I do not feel needy.

9. _____ I am not afraid of being single.

10. _____ When I am alone I do not feel lonely.

11. _____ I have an active, full life.

12. _____ When I am in an intimate relationship, I still have other interests.

13. _____ I do nice things for myself and others.

14. _____ I can receive as well as give.

15. _____ I do creative things.

16._____ I do not compare myself to others.

17._____ I can stand up for myself.

18._____ I can say "no" when it is appropriate.

19._____ I am growing and making progress in my life.

20._____ I am contributing to the world.

21._____ I have surrounded myself with healthy people.

22._____ I feel connected to myself and the world.

23._____ I feel loved by many people.

24._____ I feel like a whole person.

25._____ I do not like rejection, but I can handle it.

26._____ I do not over-react to criticism by attacking or getting defensive.

27._____ I have processed most of my feelings about my dysfunctional childhood.

28._____ I am not angry all of the time about my past.

29._____ I do not feel guilty all the time about the mistakes I have made.

30._____ I can handle adversity without falling apart.

31._____ I can end an unhealthy relationship.

32._____ I can stick with a healthy relationship.

33._____ I do not feel suicidal when relationships end.

34._____ I have some stress-management techniques.

35._____ I feel good about myself.

36._____ I know how to find balance in my life.

37._____ I know what I want, but I am not addicted to getting it.

38._____ I have structure, but I am also flexible.

39._____ I have trustworthy people in my life.

40._____ I do not have to control everything and everybody in my life.

41._____ I have worked through my sexual hangups. I know what healthy sex is.

42._____ I can argue with someone without attacking them or giving them the silent treatment.

Scoring:

0   You are *not* ready for a relationship.

0-21   You need to work on your recovery a little longer.

22-42   You are *almost* ready for a relationship.

43-62   You *are* ready but you are still vulnerable.

63-84   You are now ready for a relationship with an emotionally mature and compatible person.

Worksheet #4

Do I Have a Healthy Relationship?

Answer questions 1-21 using the following point system.

Most of the time   = 2

Some of the time   = 1

Hardly ever   = 0

In my relationship both my partner and I have:

1. _____ Honesty

2. _____ Readiness for a relationship (maturity)

3. _____ The willingness to negotiate or compromise

4. _____ Self-awareness

5. _____ Self-esteem

6. _____ Communication skills

7. _____ Sexual compatibility

8. _____ An awareness of our partner's wounded inner child

9. _____ Values similar to partner's

10. _____ Patience and tolerance

11. _____ A willingness to experience a wide range of emotions

12. _____ A willingness to let go of controlling

13. _____ A willingness to maintain our personality boundaries

14._____ Devotion

15._____ Quality time together

16._____ A healthy understanding of when to stay and when to go

17._____ Compatibility and ease

18._____ A willingness to face our problems

19._____ Respect and admiration

20._____ Reciprocity (give and take)

21._____ Realistic expectations about how much of our happiness should come from this relationship.

SCORING:

0   You *do not* have a healthy relationship.

0-11   You have some work to do.

12-21   Your relationship has a lot of potential.

22-33   Your relationship is healthy most of the time.

34-42   You have a healthy and loving relationship.

A SUMMARY OF THE ADDICTION PROCESS

Romance Addict

- The potential romance addict fantasizes a lot about romantic love and romantic rituals.

- The romance addict embraces the illusion that *only* romantic love and romantic relationships can make him or her happy.

- A dependency on fantasies and romantic love develops.

- The desire for romantic love is projected onto someone the romance addict is attracted to.

- An infatuation develops.

- A compulsive preoccupation with the loved one develops.

- A passionate affair is initiated. (Some romance addicts have more than one affair going on at the same time.)

- When the romance begins to wear off, or the honeymoon is over, the romance addict gets bored and moves on to another partner.

- The romance addict begins to feel a sense of emptiness in his or her life.

- The romance addict becomes even more preoccupied with romantic love as a "fix."

- The emotional and physical well being of the romance addict begins to deteriorate. Depression sets in.

- Other addictions progress to offset the romance addict's growing depression.

- Serious consequences can result, even death, if recovery is not initiated.

Addiction to a Person

- The potential love addict experiences a powerful attraction to someone.

- An infatuation develops (idealizing someone you don't know very well).

- Romantic love blossoms and the addiction is triggered.

- The soon-to-be love addict projects onto the loved one all of his or her dreams for eternal happiness via the reinforcing affects of romantic love.

- The love addict embraces the illusion that *only* this particular person can make them happy or satisfy their desire to love and be loved.

- The dependency deepens and a sense of "choice" disappears.

- A compulsive preoccupation with the loved one develops.

- The love addict begins to demonstrate particular forms of obsessive and distorted behavior which are symptomatic of this type of addiction (abnormal jealousy, controlling, etc.).

- If a relationship has begun, it starts to deteriorate under the stress of the love addict's obsession.

- The love addict's physical and emotional well-being begins to deteriorate.

- The obsession ends or the love addict faces serious consequences, including death.

- Another obsession begins if a program of recovery is not initiated.

Relationship Addict

- The potential relationship addict fantasizes a lot about intimate relationships.

- The relationship addict embraces the illusion that *only* intimate relationships can make him or her happy.

- A compulsive preoccupation with the idea of having a relationship develops.

- This desire for an intimate relationship becomes projected onto someone.

- A compulsive preoccupation develops.

- Once the relationship begins, the love addict begins to demonstrate particular forms of obsessive and distorted behavior which are symptomatic of this type of addiction (controlling, caretaking, clinging, accepting neglect or abuse, etc.).

- A dependency on the relationship takes root. A sense of *choice* disappears.

- The relationship starts to deteriorate under the stress of the relationship addict's obsession.

- The relationship addict's physical and emotional well-being begins to deteriorate.

- The relationship addict holds on for dear life no matter how bad the relationship gets.

- Other addictions progress to offset the relationship addict's growing depression.

- The obsession with the relationship ends or the relationship addict faces serious consequences, including death.

- Another addictive relationship begins if a program of recovery is not initiated.

Inner-Child Meditation

The following meditation is designed to help you with your reparenting. In the first part of the meditation you will meet your inner child. After you have met, you will be encouraged to *comfort* your inner child and *set limits* with him or her. You will also *make a commitment* to always be there for your inner child. Being your own parent is important. This is how you avoid becoming dependent on others in an unhealthy way. The second part of this meditation is designed to introduce you to your Higher Power. Many of you will shy away from this part of the meditation. However, note the sentiments of H. Norman Wright, in *Making Peace With the Past.*

> For some of us finding parental approval is quite impossible, because that parent is deceased or is unable to give us this gift. But the fact remains that we never outgrow our need for an accepting parent. We even parent ourselves sometimes to help us fulfill this need. But is that enough? **No!** However, realizing that God [Higher Power] is our heavenly father [parent], the kind of father a father should be, can give us deep emotional satisfaction.... *Remembering who we are in the sight of God can, in time, become a stronger force overshadowing the negative memories from the past.* [italics mine]

While the following meditation can be read (as is) to a single individual or to a mixed group of both men and women, I encourage you, when at all possible, to personalize it. For instance, if you are doing the meditation by yourself, you can give your inner child a name; or you can say "little girl" or "little boy" instead of "inner child." You can also take just one component of the meditation and focus on that, ignoring the parts that make you feel uncomfortable; or you can *add* words spontaneously to the meditation as you read it—any words that feel right to you at the time.

Get in a comfortable position. Relax and focus on your breathing.... Spend a few moments becoming mindful of your breathing.... Be aware of the air as you breathe it in and as you breath it out.... Notice the difference in the air as it comes in and as it goes out....Focus on that difference....

Now...imagine that you're walking down a long corridor. Walk down slowly as I count down from six. Six...(3 seconds). Five...(3 seconds). Four...(3 seconds), etc. As you are walking, look toward the end of the corridor. You will see a force field of light. Look at the light. It is warm and inviting. Walk toward the light.

Now, walk through the light and go back through time to a street where you lived as a child. Walk down the street until you get to one of the houses or apartments you grew up in. Look at this place. Notice the roof and the color. Notice the windows and doors. See a small child come out of the front door. This is your inner child. Look at how your child is dressed. Look at the expression on your child's face.

Walk over to your child. Tell your child that you are from the future and that you know what she (or he) has been through—all the suffering and all the loneliness. Tell your child that you have come to be a loving parent. Give your child a big hug. If your child wants to, let him or her cry in your arms and let out all of the pain. Continue comforting your child. Keep telling your child over and over again that everything is going to be all right.

Now tell your child just how wonderful he or she is. Say something like "My you are a wonderful child. I have never seen such a lovely child. I think you are just great." Keep saying this until your child gets used to it and begins to really respond. Make note of your child's response. If you do not get a positive response, make a commitment to come back and tell your child again and again just how wonderful he or she is.

As you are standing there with your child, he or she notices another child playing off in the distance. Your child asks permission to go play with this other child. Watch as your little boy or girl wanders off to play. After a moment your child returns and asks if this other child can come home to live with you. Gently tell your child that this is not possible. Encourage your child to make friends with this little boy or girl, but explain that relationships do not move this quickly. Watch your child become insistent. Continue to say "no" to your child. Explain that you are the parent and that the decision is up to you. Be kind...but stand your ground. Watch as your child accepts your decision.

It is time to go home to where you now live as an adult. Ask your inner child to go with you. (If your child will not go with you, then promise to come back and visit everyday.) If your child does agree to go with you, take him or her by the hand and start walking away from the house or apartment you grew up in. As you walk away, see your mom and dad (or the people who raised you) come out on the porch. Wave goodbye to them. Look over your shoulder as you walk away and see them getting smaller and smaller until they are completely gone.

Now, continue walking down the road holding the hand of your child. After awhile, stop to look at your child. Watch your child start to fade. Then let your child step into your body. *Now you are one and need never be separated again.*

Now, continue walking down the road. After awhile you find yourself in a lovely garden. Look at the garden. It is quiet and peaceful. There are trees and flowers. Over to the right is a sparkling brook. Suddenly you see a figure approaching from the distance. It doesn't matter whether it is a man or a woman, but you see is a look of kindness and wisdom on his or her face. After a few moments, the figure says to you "I am your Higher Power. I have taken the form of a human being so that you will not be frightened. I have come to tell you that I love you and that I am sorry for all the pain you have suffered in your life. I want you to know that everything is going to be all right.

Most of all I want you to know just how wonderful you are. You are as wonderful as anyone I know, and it makes me sad that you do not know this. Please believe me when I say that you are wonderful. I also want you to know that nothing you do will ever take away the love and respect I have for you. My love is *unconditional*."

As you listen to these words try to absorb them. They may seem contrary to what you have always believed. You may feel slightly uncomfortable.

If you believe what your Higher Power is telling you, then savor the feeling of being loved and cherished. You are hungry for this feeling. It feels good. You ask your Higher Power to stay with you always to remind you of your self-worth. Your Higher Power agrees to do this.

Now, look up into the sky. See the white clouds form the number three....Feel your stomach and your arms....See the three become a two....Feel the life in your hands, your face, your whole body....See the two become a one. Now slowly open your eyes.

THE TWELVE STEPS TO RECOVERY

What They Mean

Many people ask me whether or not I recommend 12-step programs. The answer is yes!

For those of you who don't know, the first 12-step program was Alcoholics Anonymous. After the co-founder (Bill Wilson) penned the 12-steps, they became universally accepted as an effective way to treat alcoholism. Eventually, people discovered that the 12-steps and 12-step programs were an effective way to treat other addictions as well—including addiction to love.

While 12-step *meetings* provide a supportive environment for love addicts, the heart of the program is the 12-*steps*. Any love addict attending a 12-step program should consider *working* the steps.

The 12-steps promote change by giving us tasks that can be accomplished, and by reminding us that we must *do* something in order to change.

1. We admitted we were powerless over addiction—that our lives had become unmanageable [without God].

This step introduces us to *self-honesty* and *humility*. We admit that we have a problem. We admit that we need help. This is the step of awareness. It is a preparation for inviting spiritual healing into our lives.

2. Came to believe that a Power greater than ourselves could restore us to sanity.

This step brings us *hope*. Admitting our powerlessness has deflated our ego. This can be very frightening. What shall we do if we are powerless over a life-threatening disorder? The answer to this dilemma is step two. Yes we are insane, but there is a power greater than ourselves that can take care of the problem. When we take this step, we acknowledge that spirituality can heal us. We do not have to be convinced at this point, just open-minded.

3. Made a decision to turn our will and our lives over to the care of God, as we understood God.

Healing comes from a relationship with a Higher Power. To begin this relationship we must *surrender*. The ego hates this. This surrender begins with a decision to turn our will and our life over to the care of God. This is crucial. It is like putting ourselves in the hands of a doctor once we have discovered that we have a life-threatening disease.

Note: This step can be taken even if we still have some doubts. No one is entirely convinced that this will work the first time they take this step. Later, as we get better, we will see the results of this step and it will be easier to keep making this decision to "turn it over."

4. Made a searching and fearless moral inventory of ourselves.

This step is like a *diagnosis of our problem*. When doctors are looking for a cure they begin by isolating the virus that is causing the disease. We must do the same. We must take a good hard look at ourselves. We must isolate distorted values, thoughts, and behavior. We must find and write about all the negative personality traits that cause our addiction. We must consciously define what has to be changed if we wish to heal. We must know what parts of ourselves we wish to keep and which parts we want to get rid of. Some people call the fourth step a blueprint for change.

The first time we take an inventory it is difficult to identify everything we need to know about ourselves. Don't worry about this. As we grow, more is revealed. Then we can do another fourth-step inventory. The point of the fourth step is to *practice self-honesty* and to get us into the habit of looking at ourselves with the idea of making changes. Even a short fourth-step inventory will accomplish this purpose. This step is very important.

5. Admitted to God, to ourselves, and to another human being the exact nature of our wrongs.

In this step we *share* or *confess* the negative information (wrongs) we have gathered in our fourth step. We share this information with "ourselves" (this represents self-honesty); with "God" (this represents a power greater than ourselves or, if you prefer, our unconscious); and with "another human being" (this represents the world). This step is designed to help us share our secrets. Secrets are a by-product of shame. They must come out of hiding if we are to heal. In 12-step meetings you will hear it said that we are as "sick as our secrets."

6. Were entirely ready to have God remove all these defects of character.

This step promotes *readiness*. We are reminded by this step that while we are consciously ready to have God remove all our shortcomings, we *unconsciously* cling to them out of fear and habit. When this happens we must pray for willingness. Prayer alters our unconscious reservations.

This step also reminds us that God, not us, is the one who removes defects of character from our unconscious. We learned this in the second step. We let go, but God is the power behind the changes that occur in us.

If you stumble on this step don't worry. Readiness will occur when the pain is bad enough or when your faith is strong enough. Despite the phrase "entirely ready" you can take this step with some reservations; or you can concentrate on some character defects while still clinging to others.

7. Humbly asked God to remove our shortcomings.

This gesture acknowledges the *superiority of our Higher Power*. It reminds us that he or she can do for us what we cannot do for ourselves. This step, in the form of a prayer, also helps transform our *conscious* willingness into an *unconscious* willingness. When the conscious desire becomes rooted in our unconscious we begin to change.

Just a warning: when we pray for God to remove our short-comings they will not magically disappear. God will just supply us with opportunities to make changes and hopefully we will respond with the correct behavior. God will give us a momentary reprieve from being a victim of our impulses. God will give us a sense of choice and the rest is up to us. This is how God removes shortcomings. We have to do most of the work.

8. Made a list of all persons we had harmed, and became willing to make amends to them all.

This step is designed to help us *let go of residual guilt*. It promotes *honesty* and *change*. It is an expression of our desire to put the past behind us and start over again by acknowledging the mistakes we have made. It is also a simple way to get organized for the ninth step.

9. Made direct amends to such people wherever possible, except when to do so would injure them or others.

This step is how we *implement* our desire to put the past behind us and let go of residual guilt. It is our opportunity to take action. It takes courage to take this step. This step is not designed to improve our relationship with all the people we have hurt (although it may do this). Nor will it always result in being forgiven by the people we have hurt. This step is designed to help diminish the guilt we feel. It will also help us get our self-respect back. Self-respect comes from doing the right thing even if we don't feel like it.

When taking this step we must *not* be concerned about what the person we hurt did to us either before or after we hurt them. This step is about taking responsibility for our own actions, even if what we did was a reaction to the negative deeds of someone else.

This step is also more than an apology. If we stole money, then we must return it when we can. Do not get stuck on this step. Do what you can and move on. You can come back later and work on this step some more.

10. *Continued to take personal inventory, and when we were wrong, promptly admitted it.*

This is the first of the *maintenance* steps. Like steps eleven and twelve, this step is designed to help us keep what we have gained from the first nine steps (self-respect, peace of mind, freedom from addiction, etc.) In this step we periodically access how we are doing and make note of our wrongdoings. Then we admit our mistakes and make amends. This step is crucial if we are to avoid regression.

11. *Sought through prayer and meditation to improve our conscious contact with God, as we understood God, praying only for knowledge of God's will for us and the power to carry that out.*

This step helps us *keep* and *enhance* our newfound spiritual condition. It does this by reminding us to practice spiritual disciplines. This is what keeps us in remission. Spirituality is a state of mind, but like muscles that atrophy without exercise, spirituality will grow weak without prayer, meditation, and surrendering to God's will. Prayer is *talking* to God; meditation is *listening* to God; and carrying out God's will for us is *obedience*. If you work very hard on this step, you will experience an overwhelming sense of joy and serenity.

12. *Having had a spiritual awakening as the result of these steps, we tried to carry this message to addicts, and to practice these principles in all our affairs.*

To keep what we have gotten, we have to give it away. This is a spiritual law. Bill Wilson, the co-founder of Alcoholics Anonymous, discovered this when he tried to keep Dr. Bob sober as a way of saving his own sobriety.

How does carrying the message help us? For one thing, the comfort and advice we give others comes back to us just when we need it the most. (What goes around comes around.) Also, we gain many new insights from our attempt to help others. We learn from what we teach. "To know peace we must teach peace." *A Course In Miracles*.

Helping others also makes us feel good about ourselves. This is good for our recovery. One warning with regard to this statement: Our helpfulness should be the fruit of spirituality. By this I mean that it should be genuine—come from a full heart—with no ulterior motives like trying to buy love. Also, helping others should not be done at the expense of our own well-being. There is a middle ground between selfishness and co-dependency.

There is no perfect way to "carry the message." Just do what comes naturally. Find a way that is exciting to you—sponsorship, setting up meetings, service committees, etc.

Let's not forget the second half of the twelfth step: "practice these principles in all our affairs." This statement reminds us to take what we have learned and apply it to all areas of our lives. This means taking our recovery home with us or to our job.

SUPPORT GROUP

Meeting Format

1. Let's open the meeting with a moment of silence followed by the Serenity Prayer.

   God, grant me the serenity to accept the things I cannot change, the courage to change the things I can, and the wisdom to know the difference.

2. Read the following:

   Welcome! This is a support group for men and women who want to know more about addiction to love and how to incorporate a program of recovery into their lives.

   To protect the privacy of those in attendance, please note that this meeting is closed to those not directly affected by the issues discussed. Remember that what is said in this room should remain in this room.

   For the benefit of newcomers, I would like to mention the following:

   a. This meeting is not affiliated with any other organization.

   b. We are a 24-hour support group. Please feel free to take phone numbers and call people during the week.

   c. We are self-supporting. A basket will be passed at the end of the meeting to cover the costs of rent, literature, and coffee.

   d. We will close the meeting at _____, but please feel free to stay after and continue talking on an informal basis.

3. Ask someone to read "A Brighter Tomorrow."

A BRIGHTER TOMORROW

Addiction to love does not mean falling in love with too many people or falling in love too often. It means obsessing about someone or a relationship, calling that obsession love, and allowing it to control your emotions and much of your behavior. It means realizing that your relationship is negatively affecting your health and emotional well-being, and yet finding yourself unable to let go. It means measuring the degree of your love by the depth of your pain.

Whether you have endured a long and difficult relationship with one person, or have been involved in a series of unhappy partnerships, love addicts share a common profile. This is why we have come together. In this group we will take a hard look at the reasons we go searching for the "perfect" mate and end up finding an unloving partner instead; why we have such difficulty ending relationships even though they are not meeting our needs; and how our yearning to love and be loved can so easily become an obsession. Then we will explore the possibilities for change.

Should you decide you are ready to change it will require hard work and total commitment. There are no shortcuts in recovery. Loving addictively is a pattern learned early and practiced well. To give it up will be frightening and challenging. Don't let the fear and discomfort stop you. We are here to support you on your journey; to offer understanding and guidance. We share your fears and confusion, as well as your hopes and dreams for a brighter tomorrow.

4. If this is a 12-step meeting, read the 12-steps.

5. Welcome the newcomers (if any).

6. Introduce the person giving a presentation or suggest a topic for discussion.

7. Close the meeting by asking everyone to join hands and recite, "I put my hand in yours…"

I PUT MY HAND IN YOURS

I put my hand in yours, and together we can do what we could never do alone. No longer is there a sense of hopelessness. No longer must we each depend on our own unsteady willpower. We are all together now, reaching out our hands for a power and strength greater than ours; and as we join hands we find love and understanding beyond our wildest dreams. *Keep coming back!*

Suggested Reading

Ackerman, Robert, and Susan Pickering. *Abused No More: Recovery for Women in Abusive and/or Codependent Alcoholic Relationships.* Blue Ridge Summit, PA: TAB Books, 1989.

Adams, Kenneth. *Silently Seduced: When Parents Make Their Children Partners—Understanding Covert Incest.* Deerfield Beach, Florida: Health Communications, 1992.

Appleton, William. *Fathers and Daughters.* Garden City, NY: Doubleday, 1981.

Ashner, Laurie. *When Parents Love Too Much: What Happens When Parents Won't Let Go.* New York, NY: Avon Books, 1991.

Aterburn, Stephen. *Addicted to Love: Recovery from Unhealthy Dependency in Love, Romantic Relationships and Sex.* Ann Arbor, MI: Servant Publications, 1991.

Bass, Ellen, and Laura Davis. *The Courage to Heal: A Guide for Women Surviving Child Sexual Abuse.* New York, NY: Harper and Row, 1988.

Beattie, Melody. *Codependent's Guide to the 12 Steps.* New York, NY: Prentice Hall, 1990.

Beattie, Melody. *Beyond Codependency and Getting Better All The Time.* San Francisco, CA: Harper/Hazelden, 1989.

Beattie, Melody. *Codependent No More: How to Stop Controlling Others and Start Caring For Yourself.* San Francisco, CA: Harper/Hazelden, 1987.

Berman, Steve. *The Six Demons of Love: Men's Fears of Intimacy*. New York, NY: McGraw-Hill, 1984.

Berne, Eric. *Games People Play: The Psychology of Human Relationships*. New York, NY: Grove Press, 1964.

Bireda, Martha. *Love Addiction: A Guide to Emotional Independence*. Oakland, CA: New Harbinger, 1990.

Bloomfield, Harold, and Leonard Felder. *Making Peace With Your Parents*. New York, NY: Ballantine Books, 1985.

Bradshaw, John. *Creating Love: The Next Great Stage in Growth*. New York, NY: Bantam Books, 1992.

Bradshaw, John. *Homecoming: Reclaiming and Championing Your Inner Child*. New York, NY: Bantam Books, 1990.

Bradshaw, John. *Healing The Shame That Binds You*. Deerfield Beach, Florida: Health Communications, Inc. 1988.

Bradshaw, John. *Bradshaw On The Family*. Deerfield Beach, Florida: Health Communications, Inc., 1988.

Branden, Nathaniel. *How to Raise Your Self-Esteem*. New York, NY: Bantam Books, 1987.

Branden, Nathaniel. *The Psychology of Romantic Love: Why Love Is, Why Love Is Born, Why It Sometimes Grows, Why It Sometimes Dies*. Los Angeles, CA: J.P. Tarcher, 1980.

Briggs, Dorothy. *Celebrate Yourself: Enhancing Your Own Self-Esteem*. Garden City, New York, NY: Doubleday, 1977.

Buges, Larry. *Love and Renewal: A Couple's Guide to Commitment*. Oakland, CA: New Harbinger Publications, 1990.

Burns, David. *Intimate Connection*. New York, NY: William Morrow, 1985.

Burns, David. *Feeling Good: The New Mood Therapy*. New York, NY: Morrow, 1980.

Butler, Pamela E. *Talking To Yourself*. San Francisco, CA: Harper and Row, 1983.

Carnes, Patrick. *Contrary to Love: Helping the Sexual Addict*. Minneapolis, Minnesota: CompCare Publishers, 1989.

Carnes, Patrick. *Out of the Shadows: Understanding Sexual Addiction*. Minneapolis: CompCare Publications, 1983.

Carter, Steven and Julia Sokul. *Men Who Can't Love: When a Man's Fear Makes Him Run From Commitment and What a Smart Woman Can Do About It.* New York, NY: M. Evans Co.; Berkeley Books, 1987.

Chopich, Erika and Margaret Paul. *Healing Your Aloneness: Finding Love and Wholeness Through Your Inner Child.* San Francisco, CA: Harper & Row, 1990.

Coates, Jennifer. *Women, Men & Language.* White Plains, NY: Longman, 1986.

Colgrove, Melba, Harold Bloomfield and Peter McWilliams. *How to Survive the Loss of a Love.* New York, NY: Bantam Books, 1976.

A Course In Miracles. Foundation For Inner Peace, 1975.

Covington, Stephanie. *Leaving the Enchanted Forest: The Path From Relationship Addiction.* San Francisco, CA: HarperSan Francisco, 1988.

Cowan, Connel, and Melvyn Kinder. *Women Men Love, Women Men Leave: What Makes Him Want to Commit.* New York, NY: Clarkson N. Potter, Inc., 1988.

Cowan, Connel, and Melvyn Kinder. *Smart Women, Foolish Choices: Finding the Right Man and Avoiding the Wrong Ones.* New York, NY: Clarkson N. Potter, 1985.

Cruse, Joseph: *Painful Affairs: Looking For Love Through Addiction and Codependency.* New York, NY: Doubleday, 1989.

Davidson, Joy. *The Agony of It All: The Drive For Drama and Excitement in Women's Lives.* New York, NY: Jeremy P. Tarcher, Inc., 1988.

Davis, Laura. *Allies in Healing.* New York, NY: Harper Perennial, 1991.

DeAngelis, Barbara. *Secrets About Men Every Woman Should Know.* New York, NY: Delacorte, 1990.

DeRoches, Brian. *Reclaiming Your Self: The Codependent's Recovery Plan.* New York, NY: Bantam Doubleday, 1990.

Diamond, Jed. *Looking For Love In All the Wrong Places: Overcoming Romantic and Sexual Addiction.* New York, NY: Putman, 1988.

Diamond, Jed. *Inside Out: Becoming My Own Man.* San Rafael, CA: Fifth Wave Press, 1983.

Dobson, James. *Love Must Be Tough.* (Christian literature) Word Books, 1983.

Dowling, Colette. *Cinderella Complex: Women's Hidden Fear of Independence.* New York, NY: Summit Books, 1981.

E. Blume, Sue. *Secret Survivors.* New York, NY: Wiley Books, 1990.

Evans, Patricia. *The Verbally Abusive Relationship.* Hobrook, Massachusetts: Bob Adams, Inc. 1992.

Fedders, Charlotte & Laura Elliot. *Shattered Dreams.* New York, NY: Dell Books, 1988.

Firestone, Robert W., *The Fantasy Bond: Effects of Psychological Defenses on Interpersonal Relationships.* New York, NY: Human Sciences Press, Inc., 1987.

Freedman, Rita. *Beauty Bound.* Lexington, Mass: Lexington Books, 1986.

Friedman, Sonya. *Men Are Just Desserts.* New York, NY: Warner Books, 1983.

Forward, Susan, and Craig Buck. *Obsessive Love: When Passion Holds You Prisoner.* New York, NY: Bantam Books, 1991.

Forward, Susan, and Crag Buck. *Toxic Parents.* New York, NY: Bantam Books, 1990.

Forward, Susan. *Men Who Hate Women and the Women Who Love Them.* New York, NY: Bantam Books, 1986.

Forward, Susan, and Craig Buck. *Betrayal of Innocence: Incest and Its Devastation.* Los Angeles, CA: Jeremy P. Tarcher (distributed by St. Martin's Press), 1978.

Giler, Janet, and Kathleen Neumeyer. *Redefining Mr. Right.* Oakland, CA: New Harbinger Publications, 1992.

Gilett, Richard. *Change Your Mind, Change Your World.* New York, NY: Simon and Schuster, 1992

Goldberg, Herb. *The New Male Female Relationship.* New York, NY: Morrow, 1983.

Gordon, Barbara. *I'm Dancing As Fast As I Can.* New York, NY: Harper and Row, 1979.

Gorski, Terence T. *The Players and Their Personalities: Understanding People Who Get Involved in Addictive Relationships.* Independence, MO: Herald House, 1989.

Gray, John. *Men Are From Mars and Women Are From Venus: A Practical Guide For Improving What You Want In Your Relationship.* New York, NY: Harper Collins, 1992.

Gray, John. *Men, Women and Relationships: Making Peace with the Opposite Sex.* Hillsboro, Oregon: Beyond Words Publishing, 1990.

Grizzle, Ann. *Mothers Who Love Too Much: Breaking Dependent Love Patterns in Family Relationships.* Westminister, MD: Ivy Books, 1991.

Halpern, Howard. *How to Break Your Addiction to a Person.* New York, NY: McGraw Hill, 1982.

Halpern, Howard. *Cutting Loose: An Adult Guide to Coming to Terms With Your Parents.* New York, NY: Simon and Schuster, 1976.

Harris, Thomas. *I'm O.K., You're O.K.: A Practical Guide to Transactional Analysis.* New York, NY: Harper and Row, 1969.

Hauck, Paul. *Overcoming Frustration and Anger.* Philadelphia, PA: Westminister Press, 1974.

Hendrix, Harville. *Keeping the Love You Find.* New York, NY: Pocket Books, Simon & Schuster, 1992.

Hendrix, Harville. *Getting the Love You Want: A Guide For Couples.* New York, NY: Henry Holt & Company, 1988.

Hyde, Margaret. *Sexual Abuse, Let's Talk About It.* Philadelphia, PA: Westminister Press, 1984.

Imbach, Jeff: *The Recovery of Love: Christian Mysticism and the Addictive Society.* New York, NY: The Crossroad Publishing, 1991.

Jeffers, Susan. *Feel the Fear and Do It Anyway.* San Diego, CA: Harcourt, Brace, Jovanovich, 1987.

Johnson, Robert. *We: Understanding of the Psychology of Romantic Love.* San Francisco, CA: Harper and Row, 1983.

Johnson, Spencer. *One Minute For Myself.* New York, NY: William Morrow & Co., Inc., 1985.

Kasl, Charlotte D. *Women, Sex, and Addiction: The Search for Love and Power.* San Francisco, CA: HarperSan Francisco, 1990.

Kennedy, Eugene. *If You Really Knew Me Would You Still Like Me?* Minneapolis, MN: CompCare, 1983.

Keyes, Ken. *A Conscious Person's Guide to Relationships.* St. Mary, Kentucky: Living Love Publishers (distributed by Devores), 1979.

Kid, Sue Monk. *God's Joyful Surprise: Finding Yourself Loved.* (Christian literature) San Francisco, CA: Harper & Row, 1987.

Kierkegaard, Soren. *Works of Love,* translated by Howard and Edna Hong. (Christian literature) New York, NY: Harper and Row, 1962.

Kiley, Dan. *The Wendy Dilemma.* New York, NY: Arbor House Publishers, 1984.

Kiley, Dan. *The Peter Pan Syndrome.* New York, NY: Dodd & Mead, Co., 1983.

Kingma, Daphne Rose. *Coming Apart: Why Relationships End and How to Live Through the Ending of Yours.* New York, NY: Fawcett Crest, Ballantine Books, 1987.

Kreisman, Jerold and Hal Straus, *I Hate You, Don't Leave Me: Understanding the Borderline Personality.* Los Angeles, California: Price Stern Sloan, Inc., 1989.

Larsen, Earnie. *Stage II Relationships: Love Beyond Addiction.* New York, NY: Harper and Row, 1987.

Lee, John H. *I Don't Want To Be Alone: For Men and Women Who Want to Heal Addictive Relationships.* Deerfield Beach, FL: Health Communications, 1990.

Leman, Kevin. *The Pleasers: Women Who Can't Say "No" and the Men Who Control Them.* New York, NY: Dell Publishers, 1987.

Leonard, Linda. *The Wounded Woman: Healing the Father-Daughter Relationship.* Athens, Ohio: Swallow Press, 1982.

Lerner, H. *The Dance of Intimacy.* New York, NY: Harper and Row, 1989.

Lerner, H. *The Dance of Anger: A Woman's Guide to Changing the Patterns of Intimate Relationships.* New York, NY: Harper and Row, 1985.

Lorrance, Laslow. *Love Addict at Eighty-Four: Confessions of an Old Romantic.* New York, NY: Vantage, 1991.

Love, Patricia. *The Emotional Incest Syndrome: What To Do When a Parent's Love Rules Your Life.* Bantam Books, 1990.

Ma, Anne Katherine. *Boundaries: Where You End and I Begin.* 205 West Touhy, Park Ridge, Illinois 60068, 1991.

Marlin, Emily. *Relationships in Recovery: Healing Strategies for Couples and Families.* New York, NY: Harper and Row, 1989.

May, Gerald, G. *Addiction and Grace: Love and Spirituality in the Healing of Addictions.* San Francisco, CA: HarperSan Francisco, 1991.

McKay, Matthew, and Peter Rogers, Joan Blades, Richard Gosse. *The Divorce Book.* Oakland, CA: New Harbinger Publications, 1984.

Mellody, Pia. *Facing Love Addiction: Giving Yourself the Power to Change the Way You Love.* San Francisco, CA: HarperSan Francisco, 1992.

Mellody, Pia. *Breaking Free: A Workbook for Facing Codependence.* San Francisco, CA: HarperSan Francisco, 1989.

Mellody, Pia. *Facing Codependence: What It Is, Where It Comes From and How It Sabotages Your Life.* San Francisco, CA: HarperSan Francisco, 1989.

Miller, Alice. *Drama of the Gifted Child.* New York, NY: Basic Books, 1981.

Miller, Joy. *My Holding You Up is Holding Me Back: Over Responsibility and Shame.* Deerfield Beach, Florida: Health Communications, 1991.

Miller, Joy. *Addictive Relationships: Reclaiming Your Boundaries.* Deerfield Beach, FL: Health Communications, 1989.

Missildine, W. Hugh. *Your Inner Child of the Past.* New York, NY: Simon & Schuster, 1963.

Moustakas, Clark. *Portraits of Loneliness and Love:* New York, NY: Prentice Hall, 1990.

Moustakas, Clark. *Loneliness and Love:* New York, NY: Prentice Hall, 1974.

Moustakas, Clark. *Loneliness.* New York, NY: Prentice Hall, 1961.

Nakken, Craig. *The Addictive Personality: Roots, Rituals and Recovery.* Center City, MN: Hazelden, 1988.

NiCarthy, Ginny. *Getting Free: A Handbook for Women in Abusive Relationships.* Seattle, Oregon: Seal Press, 1982.

Norwood, Robin. *Letters From Women Who Love Too Much: A Closer Look at Relationship Addiction and Recovery.* New York: NY Simon & Schuster, 1988.

Norwood, Robin. *Women Who Love Too Much: When You Keep Wishing and Hoping He'll Change.* New York, NY: Pocket Books, 1985.

Oliver-Diaz, Philip, and Patricia A. O'Gorman. *Twelve Steps to Self Parenting.* Deerfield Beach, Florida: Health Communications, 1988.

Paul, Jordan and Margaret Paul. *From Conflict to Caring.* Minneapolis, MN: CompCare Publishers, 1988.

Paul, Jordan, and Margaret Paul. *Do I have to Give Up Me to Be Loved By You?* Allen, Texas: Argus Communications, 1975.

Pearson, Carol. *The Hero Within.* San Francisco, CA: Harper and Row, 1986.

Peck, Scott. *The Road Less Traveled: A New Psychology of Love, Traditional Values, and Spiritual Growth.* New York, NY: Simon and Schuster, 1978.

Peele, Stanton. *Love and Addiction.* New York, NY: New American Library, 1975.

Person, Ethel, M. *Dreams of Love & Fateful Encounters.* (Mature love vs. romantic love.) New York, NY: Viking-Penguin, 1989.

Peterson, Sylvia Ogden. *From Love That Hurts to Love That's Real.* (*Recovery workbook.*) Park Ridge, Illinois: Parkside Publishing Corporation, 1989.

Phelps, Janice Keller, and Alan E. Nourse. *The Hidden Addictions and How To Get Free.* New York, NY: Little, Brown, and Co, 1986.

Phillips, Debora with Robert Judd. *How to Fall Out of Love.* New York, NY: Warner Books, 1978.

Reynolds, David. *Playing Ball on Running Water*. New York, NY: William Morrow and Co., 1984.

Ricketson, Susan C. *Dilemma of Love: Healing Codependent Relationships at Different Stages of Life*. Deerfield Beach, FL: Health Communications, 1990.

Rosselini, Gayle, and Mark Worden. *Here Comes the Sun: Dealing With Depression*. Center City, MN: Hazelden, 1987.

Rosselini, Gayle, and Mark Worden. *Of Course You're Angry*. Center City, MN: Hazelden, 1985.

Rubin, Lillian. *Intimate Strangers*. New York, NY: Harper and Row, 1983.

Rubin, Theodore Isaac. *The Angry Book*. New York, NY: MacMillan, 1969.

Russianoff, Penelope. *Why Do I Think I'm Nothing Without a Man*. New York, NY: Bantam Books, 1982.

Sanford, Linda Tschirhart, and Mary Ellen Donovan. *Women and Self-Esteem*. New York, NY: Penguin Books, 1985.

Sandvig, Karen J. *Growing Out of An Alcoholic Family: Overcoming Addictive Patterns in Alcoholic Family Relationships*. Ventura, CA: Regal, 1990.

Schaef, Ann. *Escape From Intimacy, Untangling the Love Addictions: Sex, Romance, Relationships*. San Francisco, CA. Harper and Row, 1989.

Schaef, Ann. *Co-Dependence: Misunderstood-Mistreated*. Minneapolis, MN: Winston Press, 1986.

Scarf, Maggie. *Intimate Partners: Patterns in Love and Marriage*. New York, NY: Random House, 1987.

Schaeffer, Brenda. *Is It Love, Or Is It Addiction?* Center City, MN: Hazelden, 1987.

Seabury, David. *The Art of Selfishness*. New York, NY: J. Messner, Inc. 1937.

Seixas, Judith and Geraldine Youcha. *Children of Alcoholism: A Survivors Manual*. New York, NY: Crown Publishers, 1985.

Shain, Merle. *When Lovers Are Friends*. Philadelphia, PA: Lippincott, 1978.

Sills, Judith. *Excess Baggage: Getting Out of Your Own Way; Overcoming the Blind Spots That Make Your Life Harder Than It Has to Be*. New York, NY: Viking Press, 1993.

Sills, Judith. *A Fine Romance: The Passage of Courtship Meeting to Marriage*. New York, NY: Ballantine Books, 1987.

Sills, Judith. *How to Stop Looking For Someone Perfect and Find Someone to Love*. New York, NY: Ballatine Books, 1984.

Smedes, James B. *Forgiving and Forgetting*. San Francisco, CA: Harper and Row, 1984.

Smith, Manuel. *When I Say No I Feel Guilty*. Los Angeles, CA: Pacifica Foundation, 1975.

Somers, Suzanne. *Keeping Secrets*. New York, NY: Warner Books, 1988.

Tannen, Deborah. *You Just Don't Understand: Women and Men in Conversation*. New York, NY: Morrow, 1990.

Tannen, Deborah. *That's Not What I Mean: How Conversational Style Makes or Breaks a Relationship*. New York, NY: Ballantine Books, 1986.

Taylor, Cathryn. *The Inner Child Workbook: What to Do With Your Past When it Won't Go Away*. Los Angeles, CA: Jeremy P. Tarcher, Perigee Books, 1991.

Walker, Lenore. *The Battered Woman*. New York, NY: Harper and Row, 1979.

Wakerman, Elyce. *Father Loss: Daughters Discuss The Man That Got Away*. Garden City, NY: Doubleday, 1984.

Wegscheider-Cruse, Sharon. *Coupleship: How to Build a Relationship*. Deerfield Beach, Florida: Health Communications, 1988.

Wegscheider-Cruse, Sharon. *Learning to Love Yourself*. Deerfield Beach, Flordia: Health Communications, Inc., 1987.

Wegscheider-Cruse, Sharon. *Choicemaking for Co-dependents, Adult Children, and Spirituality Seekers*. Pompano Beach, Florida: Health Communications, Inc., 1985.

Weinhold, Barry. *Breaking Free of Addictive Family Relationships*. Dallas, TX: Stillpoint, 1991.

Welwood, John. *Journey of the Heart: Intimate Relationships and the Path of Love.* New York, NY: Harper Perennial, 1991.

Welwood, John. *Challenge of the Heart: Love, Sex, & Intimacy In Changing Times.* Boston, MA: Shambhala Publications; New York, NY: Distributed in U.S. by Random House, 1985.

Whitfield, Charles. *Healing the Child Within: Discovery and Recovery For Adult Children of Dysfunctional Families.* Pompano Beach, Florida: Health Communications, 1987.

Wholey, Dennis. *Becoming Your Own Parent.* New York, NY: Doubleday, 1988.

Woititz, Janet. *Struggle For Intimacy.* Pompano Beach, Florida: Health Communications, 1985.

Woititz, Janet. *Adult Children of Alcoholics.* Pompano Beach, Florida: Health Communications, 1983.

Womack, William. *The Marriage Bed: Renewing Love, Friendship, Trust, and Romance.* Oakland, CA: New Harbinger Publications, 1991.

Wood, Barbara. *Children of Alcoholism: The Struggle For Self and Intimacy in Adult Life.*

Wright, H. Norman. *Making Peace With the Past.* (Christian literature) Old Tappan, New Jersey: H. Revell Co., 1985.

Zerof, Herbert. *Finding Intimacy: The Art of Happiness In Living Together.* New York, NY: Random House, 1978.

An Irish Blessing

May the road rise to meet you.
May the wind be always at your back,
The sun shine warm upon your face,
The rain fall soft upon your fields,
And until we meet again
May God hold you in the hollow of His hand.